W9-AZS-188

SILVER LININGS

Stories for the

Christian Spirit

Trusting in God's Plan

Publications International, Ltd.

Cover illustration: Linda Montgomery

Illustrators: Vivian Browning, Marian Hirsch, Steven Mach, Linda Montgomery

Scripture quotations are from the *New Revised Standard Version* of the Bible, copyright © 1989, by the Division of Christian Education of the National Council of the Churches of Christ in the United States of America, and are used by permission. All rights reserved. Marked translations are *New International Version* (NIV) *King James Version* (KJV), and *The Living Bible* (TLB).

Louis Weber, CEO
Publications International, Ltd.
7373 North Cicero Avenue
Lincolnwood, Illinois 60712

Permission is never granted for commercial purposes.

Manufactured in China.

8 7 6 5 4 3 2 1

ISBN: 0-7853-3993-0

Library of Congress Card Number: 00-110346

Contents

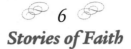

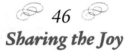
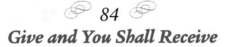
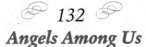

Stories of Faith

A house, experts agree, is only as good as its foundation. So, too, it is with our lives.

It's best for both houses and lives to begin with a strong foundation. God is the master builder. He created the blueprint for every one of us, using Jesus as the rock upon which to build.

This book invites us into the lives of remarkable people who've experienced God's creative, uplifting presence and discovered his blueprint for their lives. Their stories will transform and inspire you.

Through words and images, you will be reminded that God knows each of us and wants only the best for us. These stories remind us that ours is a steadfast God, to whom we can always turn for comfort and inspiration. Our God is not the author of troubles, but rather the source of strength and hope.

Throughout our journey, we are nurtured and strengthened by family ties, steadfast friendships, and life within a community—especially the fellowship of faith. God, as we are told by those who've come to know firsthand, is constantly using people in our lives to inspire, support, and guide us.

As a parent guides a child, so God directs us, showing us a better way. We can take heart knowing that we can turn our woeful, misshapen lives over to the Great Redeemer, who transforms us into something constructive.

This transforming act can create powerful changes in our lives—and the lives of others—as our words and actions travel like ripples in a pond, touching and inspiring others.

Take a quiet moment, close your eyes, and listen. You can hear a still, small voice in the midst of our hectic world, which often seems more determined to knock us down like a wrecking ball rather than build us up. That voice is God calling you: "I have called you by name, you are mine" (Isaiah 43:1).

Indeed, we are claimed as God's own and he knows us by name. This is a foundation we can trust. A foundation upon which we can build our lives. You are invited to consider the stories presented here. Encouragement, joy, comfort, blessing, guidance...these are gifts to help us build on God's design for abundant life. These gifts are shared here by many people whose stories he made possible.

Faith is the ear of the soul.

—CLEMENT OF ALEXANDRIA

The Voice of God

Letters From God

Weakened by old age, Sarah thought she was no longer capable of helping others or serving God. But then she got an idea...

Somehow living alone wasn't all Sarah had expected it to be. After all those years busily caring for her family, she thought how wonderful it would be to have time to herself, to relax and focus on her own needs. And now, here she was, with very little to do, very little she felt strong enough, well enough to do.

At her age, she wasn't feeling up to taking long trips or exploring new places.

Besides, she'd always done something meaningful, something for others. She'd helped out in the church nursery for years, until her back started aching so badly. At her age, her energy dropped so quickly. She tired quickly. There were so many things she didn't feel up to doing anymore. But she missed the activity, the involvement, being there for people, serving God, reaching out to others.

She'd gotten so weak and shaky, she felt irritable with herself.

"You're useless," she accused her own face looking back at her from the mirror. What could she do to help others? What good was she anymore to God or anybody else? Perhaps she'd just settle in front of the TV and dwindle away. Perhaps there wouldn't be anything more she could do for God or others. Perhaps her usefulness had truly ended.

But one day, she picked up the paper to leaf through it. There wasn't much worth reading— so much bad news, so much pain and sorrow. Some days it made her heart ache just browsing through the pages. So much trouble in the world. If only there were something she could do to help.

Then she spotted the photo. That poor family, stranded far from home, half of them in a hospital from a serious car wreck, not knowing anybody, no resources, no help. She studied the photo again and again, feeling deeply touched by the family and their plight. Even after setting aside the newspaper, she couldn't stop thinking about them and what they were going through. But what could she do? They were total strangers and far away from where she lived. Not a thing she could do for them.

But they wouldn't leave her thoughts. She saw their faces in her mind throughout the day. She felt the strongest push inside to do something for them. She just had no idea what to do. Then it came to her, clear as anything. She rushed for her stationery box and began to write. She sent them a letter, full of kind words and encouragement, and promised that she would be praying for them all. She reminded them that God would not forget them and would never leave them.

She tucked in a few scripture tracts, then sealed and mailed the letter. Such a warm rush of peace flowed through her. It was exactly the right thing to do. She felt God's presence coursing through her. And because she meant her promise to pray for them, she cut out that newspaper photo and tacked it to her bulletin board as a prayer reminder. But while going through the paper again, she came upon another moving story with a photo attached. Another difficult situation with people hurting and alone. Thinking it over, Sarah pulled out her stationery and set to work again.

She probably would never hear from these people. She'd never know whether her letter helped or not, but she felt a certainty that she was doing something meaningful, something right, something God wanted her to do.

And before she knew it, the job took a strong hold on her life. Just about every day now she was writing letters to complete strangers, people suffering from trials and troubles, people who needed a kind, encouraging word. She started stockpiling greeting cards to send as well. Soon her days were full again.

She had never felt busier, or happier, or more content. She knew she was exactly where God wanted her to be. There wasn't a whole lot she could do, but this one thing she could do, and she could do it eagerly. Soon her bulletin board was so full, she had to cover an entire wall with corkboard. Several friends and neighbors heard of her efforts and joined her.

A group of them met regularly to pray for their unknown friends. Some of them even sent contributions of food, clothing, or cash whenever a family or individual was in dire need. Sarah lifted her head from prayer one day to look around at the group around her, at the busy activity of helping others, and her heart rejoiced.

Perhaps at her age there wasn't a whole lot she could still do, but she could write these "letters from God." She could obey his direction for her life. She no longer felt alone and empty, as if her life was over, and she realized, in a way, the letters had changed her life as much as they had touched anybody else's.

—KAREN M. LEET

I call upon you, for you will answer me, O God; incline your ear to me, hear my words.

—PSALM 17:6

An Honest Reward

After resisting temptation, Yvette discovered a great sense of peace—and other rewards.

To a young mother trying to make ends meet, every dollar counted. Even with her husband working full-time, and the small income she made doing daycare, Yvette still could not pay the bills on time.

This month was no exception, with her checkbook showing that unless $250 materialized in the next two days, rent would be late again. And this time the landlord had promised to evict. Discouraged, Yvette closed her eyes and prayed, asking God for guidance. She was startled as her seven-year-old son, Jansen, came running through the door. He excitedly handed his mother a man's leather wallet he had found on the way home from school. Yvette looked inside, where she discovered a photo of a little girl, a note written in crayon, and $300 in cash!

Maybe this is the miracle I was just praying for, she thought. But as she held the cash, a feeling of discomfort stirred deep within her. She found herself instead calling the local police department. One hour later, she and Jansen handed the wallet to a police officer, who told them that if it were not claimed within a few days, the money would be theirs.

Yvette felt such a sense of peace and certainty as they left the station. The money was not hers, and she could not in good conscience pretend otherwise. On the drive home, she explained to Jansen that her faith in God was stronger than her temptation to do something she clearly knew was wrong.

Two days later, as Yvette prepared to visit the landlord with only half of the rent, she was delayed by a knock on her door. She opened it and smiled at the kindly old man holding the leather wallet in his hand. He began thanking Yvette profusely, and when he offered her a large monetary reward, she almost fainted. Naturally, she refused to take it, but the man insisted. He took out the photo of the little girl, and the note scrawled in crayon, and explained that it was the last note his granddaughter ever wrote him before she died of leukemia. That note meant everything to him,

and he was grateful that Yvette had the integrity
to do the right thing.

That month the rent was paid on time, and
Yvette even had some money to spare. God
truly did take care of her and her family, even if
it was in the most mysterious of ways.

—MARIE JONES

In Stillness

I know that faith is what keeps
   me moving forward.
But sometimes, too, my trust
   allows a leisure like this.
For you, God, are the one who
   upholds all things.
Even as I sit here in stillness,
your breath keeps me breathing,
your mind keeps me thinking,
your love keeps me yearning for
   home.

Lord, Are You There?

"We know that all things work together for good for those who love God, who are called according to his purpose."

ROMANS 8:28

*I*t happened when I was on my knees in church pouring my heart out to God. Tears were streaming down my face as I begged God to help. My problems were overwhelming me, and I felt like I couldn't handle them anymore. So I came to church and I wept.

Then a small inward voice said, "Go see Jane." I brushed it away, but it came through even more loudly: "Go see Jane." I thought, *Jane who?* Immediately I remembered a woman I had met about two years earlier. I barely knew her and, even though I knew where she lived, I didn't even know her last name.

Why? was my next thought. No answer came, just, "Go see Jane."

Jane lived an hour and a half away. What reason would I give my husband for making such a trip? I couldn't say, "Oh, by the way, Bill, I have to go to Scottsdale because God wants me to see Jane." Imagine his reaction to that!

When was I supposed to go? Next week would be soon enough, I thought. But the Lord immediately convinced me that next week was too late.

Was there enough gasoline in my car? Was there any money to buy gas? All sorts of questions haunted me. Finally I agreed to go, but God would have to work out the details. After reminding God not to forget my own prayers, I told him I would go see Jane, and then I went home.

We had moved away from Scottsdale over a year earlier, but our house still sat empty and unsold. Checking on the house would be a good excuse to make the trip. I had enough money for gasoline and a little extra to buy lunch.

The next day, I drove to Jane's house. It was a beautiful, warm, sunny day. As I drove, I prayed and I worried. Had God really told me to go see Jane, or was I just so distraught that I imagined it? What should I say when I knocked on her door? The answer came just as fast as the thought. I will tell her the truth. I will say exactly what happened, and if she thought I was crazy, then so be it. But what if she wasn't home? If she's not home, then I will know God had not sent me, but I will have shown my willingness to be obedient.

I checked on our old house, then drove to Jane's. As I pulled into her driveway, my heart did flip-flops. My whole body trembled, and I sat in the car for a couple minutes to calm myself. Thoughts whirled through my mind.

She's going to think I'm crazy—but I know God is sending me to her. . . . I could drive away right now, and she will never know it. . . . But God will know, and if he really did send me, how will I face him? Can I say to him, "I'm afraid to trust you"?

"Well," I finally said to myself, "I may never see her again, anyway. So just do it."

I got out of the car and walked up to the house. I prayed as I knocked on the screen door. I could see Jane inside. She had a telephone tucked under her ear and was talking in low tones. As she walked toward the door, she motioned for me to give her a minute.

She was much thinner than I remembered. I backed away from the door to give her a moment and heard her end the conversation.

When she came outside, I knew instantly that all was not well. Her appearance was neat and clean, but her face was filled with sadness. She said hello and commented that my family had moved away some time ago. She wondered what I was doing back in Scottsdale.

In a somewhat brave voice, I said, "You may not believe this, but I was praying in church the other day and God said, 'Go see Jane.'"

Raising her eyebrows, she asked, "What?"

With less courage than I'd originally intended, and my eyes focused on the ground, I repeated what I had said. She recognized my discomfort and replied, "Yes, I believe you, I believe you. I can't believe it, but I do believe it. I have prayed for someone to talk to. I haven't been able to eat or sleep for three days. All I have done is cry and pray. I'm in a real mess, and I don't know what to do. I need someone to talk to. I can't talk to my family or my friends about this." She motioned toward the

porch steps and invited me to sit down. She talked and I listened. Several times she stopped and asked what I thought she should do. I had no answers.

God had sent me, but he hadn't provided any further instructions. The only thing that came to my mind was a scripture passage about all things working together for good if we love God. Jane wanted to hear again how God had called me to come visit her. We shared stories and talked about books we had read about how God answers prayers. Before leaving, I gave her a hug. She thanked me for coming, and we marveled at how really wonderful God is.

On the drive home, I became overjoyed at the realization of what God had done. I no longer felt engulfed with my own problems— or even Jane's, for that matter. I knew I didn't need to worry. God was in charge, and he would take care of everything! For the first time in my life, I had complete assurance that God was alive and that he was using me. Imagine that! He chose to use *me*. I thanked him and praised him, and I laughed and sang all the way home.

A month later, I made another trip to Scottsdale to see how Jane was doing. I pulled into her driveway, but I could see that she had moved, disappeared. Again I realized I didn't know her last name.

On my drive home, I thought about the entire episode. I know that it's not important for me to understand what happened to Jane. God knows where she is and what she is doing, and since he cared enough to send me to see her, I know that he is taking care of her. What was important for me to learn is that God listens and cares and gets involved in our lives. God could have helped Jane in so many ways. I feel blessed that he trusted me enough to use me in his plan.

—ELAINE MITCHELL

For you, O Lord, are my hope,
my trust, O Lord, from my youth.

—PSALM 71:5

This One Day

"This is the day which the Lord has made; we
will rejoice and be glad in it."
PSALM 118:24

James planned to start painting the house.
He'd put it off and put it off until it was
almost too late, and he definitely had to get it
done. But as he gathered painting supplies, he
couldn't stop thinking about his mother.
Thoughts of her kept creeping into his mind,
distracting him, tugging at his attention.
Maybe something was wrong with her, he
thought. Getting up in years and living by
herself...sometimes it worried all of them. So,
he set aside his brushes and rollers to give her a
quick call.

"I'm fine, hon," she assured her son, but
something still nagged at him, giving him no
peace, and finally he spoke up, surprising himself with his suggestion.

"Hey, Mom, do you think you feel up to an
outing?" he asked, astounded at himself. He
had things to do, but he couldn't seem to focus
anyway. "Why don't we fix a picnic and spend
the day at the park?"

"Are you sure you've got time?" she asked, and James insisted that he did. All thoughts of painting were bumped right from his head. This felt right, strong and sure.

As he gathered up his wife and kids, Frisbees and picnic basket, the phone rang.

"Hey, James." His youngest sister, Megan, was calling. "Listen, I can't stop thinking about Mom and about how alone she must feel since we're all gone from home now. I was thinking maybe we could do something together."

"Join the party," he told her, laughing, as he explained their impromptu outing. Megan eagerly agreed to drop her plans for the day. "It's nothing I can't postpone," she said, and was ready in hardly any time at all.

By the time they were ready to leave for the park, James heard from his brother and other two sisters. Somehow they'd all been thinking about Mom, thinking about her living alone, and about how they didn't get to see her often enough. The next thing any of them knew, they were having a good old-fashioned family gathering, all of them and their families.

Mom was in seventh heaven. She grinned until she claimed her face would split wide open.

"It's so good to all be together," she kept saying, enjoying everything. She applauded the tug-of-war and laughed over the kids' muddy clothing afterward. She ate her fill of peanut butter sandwiches and cheered on the family softball game. She got reacquainted with all of her grandchildren, learning about their grades in school, their friends, their interests.

"This is the best idea you've ever had," Megan told James during a lull, as they all lounged around resting. "Mom is loving every moment. We should do this more often."

"Yeah, if we weren't all so busy," James said with a shrug. "In fact, it's amazing to get all of us together at one time and in one place on such short notice."

The more James thought about it, the more amazing it seemed. His brother and sisters were always busy, with families, jobs, household

chores, church activities, and on and on. Getting together like that was some kind of minor miracle. But it was great. He hadn't seen Mom enjoy herself so much in years. He felt grateful he'd listened to that urge to drop everything and spend time with Mom. He felt deep gratitude that his brother and sisters had done the same, that they'd felt the same strong urge.

Then their wonderful day together was done. James drove his mother home and smiled, listening as she talked about what a great time she'd had.

"It was the best gift ever," she told him. "You couldn't have done anything I'd like better. It was so good to be with all of you, to see you all enjoying yourselves together, to be one big family having fun. Thank you so much for getting it started, son."

They hugged, and James drove home to get back to his normal chores and responsibilities. Life seemed busier than ever. Two days later, he felt a new gratitude for their time together. His mother had died quietly in her sleep, and the family gathered again to make plans for the funeral.

Amid their grief and sense of loss, every one of them talked about the wonderful memories they'd have of that last picnic in the park. Every one of them had stories to share and photos as mementos. Every one of them felt immense gladness to have had that special time together with their mother before her death.

And every one of them wondered if the timing of their get-together was a coincidence ... or, perhaps, a gift from God.

—KAREN M. LEET

We Trust

I falter where I firmly trod,
And falling with my weight of cares
Upon the great world's altar stairs
That slope through darkness up
    to God,

I stretch lame hands of faith,
    and grope,
And gather dust and chaff, and call
To what I feel is Lord of all,
And faintly trust the larger hope.

—ALFRED, LORD TENNYSON

Angels in the Making

Were Bobby and Raymond too young to delight in the joy of giving? Their parents were in for a surprise.

*J*oe and I wanted our two young boys to be raised with strong values and an appreciation of service. Thanksgiving was approaching, and Joe suggested that instead of the usual noisy family bash, we should go down to the local mission and help serve meals to the city's homeless.

Needless to say, Bobby and Raymond hated the idea. But Joe and I insisted, and we herded two disappointed little boys into the car and headed for St. Joseph's, where several hundred homeless families would receive a rare hot dinner. On the way, we tried to explain what generosity meant, but by the looks on their young faces, our message held little impact.

When we got to the mission, Bobby and Raymond were given the job of handing out plates of cornbread. We watched as they walked the aisles of picnic tables that had been set up, barely speaking a word except to each other. Joe and I served turkey and fixings, and when we next looked up, the boys were in a corner look-ing bored and tired. Still, they had more work to do; an adult volunteer handed them napkins to pass out.

After a few hours, I told Joe I would check on the boys. When I did, I was surprised to find them chatting with a homeless family. Ray-mond came up to me and whispered sadly that he didn't know there were so many kids with-out nice houses.

After a long day, we headed home. The boys were quiet and eventually fell asleep in the back-seat. As days went by, they said little about their Thanksgiving experience. Joe and I wondered if maybe they were just too young to understand what it meant to serve others. The spirit of giving was something they would grow into, Joe said. We just had to give them time.

As Christmas approached, I promised the boys we would spend it at home. Imagine my surprise when they protested! They not only *wanted* to return to the mission for the holiday, but they had been busy preparing gifts and drawings for all the new friends they had made! No wonder they were so quiet. The boys even gathered gifts of toys they no longer used for the children. We spent that Christmas Eve alone, but on Christmas Day we headed down to St. Joe's and served up meals, smiles, and gifts made by two "angels in the making."

—MARIE JONES

A life of faith … enables us
to see God in everything and
it holds the mind in a state
of readiness for whatever
may be his will.

—FRANÇOIS FENELON

An Answer to a Stranger's Prayer

When God calls on you to spread his word, your mission field may be closer than you think!

*E*va restlessly paced her living room floor. She couldn't get to sleep. Her family was besieged with health and financial problems, and no solutions seemed to be in sight. Eva was a churchgoing woman, but lately it seemed that her prayers were just empty, powerless words. Could God hear her cries of pain? Did he care? Was God even real?

Eva's faith had never been so low in all of her 50-some years of life. Her thoughts turned to Larry, her missing ex-husband. Neither she nor her family had heard from him in over ten years. Was he still alive, she wondered, or had the alcohol finally killed him like it had killed their marriage? Eva had never remarried, and her love for Larry had gradually faded to concern. After all, he was the father of her only child, Larry Jr.

Larry Jr. was a father himself now, with a precious little boy who had never seen his grandfather. Eva sighed. Maybe it was for the better, but still . . . she couldn't help but wonder what had happened to her ex-husband. She chided herself for her lack of faith. God was the only hope she had. Finally, she laid back on the couch in her Anderson, South Carolina, home and stared up at the ceiling.

"Dear Lord," she prayed, "please let our family know if Larry is alive or not."

She knew her only son needed to know if his father was still living. At one time her son was planning to go into the ministry, and he'd even attended a Christian college for a few years, but he eventually fell away from God. The problems their family suffered only seemed to cement Larry Jr.'s belief that God was remote and uncaring. Now only God and a mother's prayers could provide the answers the family needed.

Little did Eva know that God was already arranging an answer to her prayer, hundreds of miles away.

That same evening, my husband, Kevin, and I were walking down the streets of the historic French Quarter in New Orleans, enjoying a much-needed vacation. The sun was rapidly fading behind the clouds, and we quickened our step to reach the hotel before dark. The streets that had seemed quite safe in the daylight were now becoming bedrooms for the homeless.

As Kevin discussed his plans to lead a group of teenagers on a missionary trip to Quito, Ecuador, the following summer, I began to feel God tugging at my heart. The more my husband talked about the evangelistic crusade, the heavier my heart felt. I suddenly stopped on the sidewalk and turned toward my husband.

"Kevin, I feel so guilty. Here we're talking about witnessing to the people in South America, but look at all these homeless people we're walking by that also need to know about God's love."

Kevin looked around and then back at me. It was as if he had been so engrossed in his conversation that he hadn't even seen the people bedding down in the street. They were such a common sight in the French Quarter that after awhile they became almost invisible. As tourists, we'd been cautioned to walk quickly past the homeless and to stay off the streets after dark. We had heard horror stories of muggings—and worse—that others had suffered who hadn't heeded this rule. But that night there was a divine plan in motion that not even fear could stop.

"You're right," Kevin said soberly. "Let's stop and talk to the next homeless person we see."

With hearts pounding, the two of us walked forward in the fading light. Ahead, a man wearing ragged clothes sat on a trash can outside of a bar. As we drew closer, we heard the man calling out for money. Most people walked quickly past him, looking away, but when he spoke to us, we smiled at him encouragingly.

We soon discovered that the man was drunk and very talkative. We asked general questions about him and his life, but we waited to reveal that we were Christians. I silently prayed for God to give us the opening we needed.

Suddenly, I couldn't believe my ears. The hair on my arm stood straight up as I heard the man, whose name was Larry, tell me about his son, Larry Jr., who had attended a Christian college in Tennessee.

"Why, my husband and I both went to that college!" I exclaimed. "When did your son attend?"

Larry scratched his unshaven chin and thought. "It was in the early '80s."

I was dumbfounded. "That's when we attended," I said. "What is your son's name?"

Larry replied, "Larry Grimm, Jr."

The name rang a bell in our memories. What were the odds of this happening? There were less than 1,000 students who attended the college during that time. We both knew it had to be God who had divinely orchestrated this moment.

The longer we talked, the more sober Larry became. We bought him dinner and talked with him about the Lord. We learned that he had been living on the street and hadn't talked to his family in ten years. Hours later, we prayed the prayer of salvation with him.

When we returned to our Florida home a few days later, I immediately contacted the college's alumni association for Larry Jr.'s last known address. Then I called the Anderson, South Carolina, number that the college had provided. After a few rings, a woman answered.

"You don't know me," I began excitedly, "but I'm calling to tell you that last Thursday night we met a man who I believe is your ex-husband."

The woman on the other end of the phone began to sob.

After I told her about the encounter with her husband, Eva told me how, on that same evening, she had prayed for God to let her know if Larry was alive.

"Now I know that God really does hear and answer my prayers," she exclaimed. "My son will know where his father is and that he is still alive."

Eva explained the difficulties her family had endured and how they had begun to wonder if God really cared. We prayed together over the phone, and she told me that this experience would give her the strength to keep going and to trust in God again. I realized then how important it is to respond to those tuggings in my heart, since I never know who or what I might find at the other end of the heartstrings.

—REGINA M. BALLARD

God Said Go

What do you do when God urges you to visit your old friend? You just go.

I was busy, things to do, always more things to do. I felt even more behind than usual that morning, so when a sudden urge nudged me, I resisted. I had chores that couldn't be put off, responsibilities, business. But I couldn't push the thought away. I kept thinking about a friend. No matter what I did, she kept popping into my mind.

I started my morning chores and kept trying to ignore the nagging little voice in the back of my head, but I couldn't. The pressure just kept getting stronger and stronger. I kept thinking about my friend, feeling uneasy, propelled to see her.

Since it was early, I told myself I'd wait awhile, then give her a quick call, just to say "hi." That was all I planned to do. But I couldn't put my mind at rest. It didn't feel right waiting. And it didn't feel right to just call. I actually reached for the phone, but I couldn't bring myself to dial her number. For one thing, she might still be in bed. I was an early riser, but that didn't mean everybody was. I tended to think my friend liked to sleep.

So, I kept telling myself that I was being silly, foolish, stupid. That I needed to stop letting myself be distracted and settle down to routine. I kept promising to call her later, to maybe fix up a small thinking-of-you gift, to perhaps pop some muffins in the oven to take to her later.

But it wouldn't do. Nothing would do except to go see her right that very moment. I didn't want to go. I'd feel ridiculous just showing up on her doorstep this early. And what would I say to her? There was no sane reason to do this. But I couldn't fight it a moment longer. I put aside everything I was doing and headed for the door.

Ignoring the feeling of being silly, I marched to her house and knocked on her door. She answered looking half asleep, rumpled, startled. But she invited me inside. I couldn't think of an excuse, so I didn't offer one. We sat at her kitchen table and chatted awhile. We sipped coffee and ate slightly stale coffee cake. We started talking about deeper things, about worries and troubles.

She spoke of some heavy problems facing her, things that felt overwhelming, that she couldn't even begin to handle. And so we talked and prayed together. We hugged and felt closer than ever before. We even finally found laughter in spite of the difficulties looming in our lives.

We spent some time reading together from our Bibles, encouraging each other. I felt so much better, lighter, freer, as if a great weight had been lifted from my heart. Perhaps that's why God had sent me so early in the morning. Perhaps it was just what I needed, to spend this close time with my friend. Perhaps my whole day would go so much smoother for the closeness we'd shared over coffee at her table.

Her weariness seemed lessened. Even her tousled hair looked better after our time together. I was so glad I had stopped ignoring that nudge to go spend time with her. Just talking on the phone wouldn't have been the same. It was time well spent for us both. Then it was time to leave. It felt right.

At the door, she stopped me a moment. "Why'd you come over today?" she wanted to know.

I shrugged, not totally certain myself. But to be honest, I had to tell her. "I felt a nudge," I said, "a push to come, from God I think. It was as if he sent me, as if he insisted I come over right at that very instant." I smiled, feeling a bit embarrassed but knowing I'd done the right thing.

She looked deep into my eyes, a gaze that unnerved me, as if she knew something I didn't know.

"I'm glad God sent you," she told me, her eyes still so very serious that it made me uncomfortable. What was going on here? Why did she seem so serious, so impressed by my urge to come?

She pulled something out of her pocket and put it in my hand. I looked down at the small, plastic container cradled in my palm, then looked back at my friend's serious face. The pills rattled in their bottle as I trembled.

"If you hadn't come . . ." she said, but did not finish her sentence. Tucking the bottle in my own pocket, I hugged her tighter than ever.

My friend, I might have lost her. It shook me realizing how close she'd come to despair.

In that moment, I resolved not to ignore God's directions in my life again. If he said to go, then I would go whether I understood the reasons or not.

—KAREN M. LEET

Promises Faithfully Kept

Faith is not just about believing in God. It's about believing he'll do what he says—that he'll keep every promise he's made in the Holy Bible. When we are faithful, like God, we keep the promises we make. And when we have faith in another person, we believe they will keep the promises they have made.

Understanding Atonement

I was not there when Jesus Christ died,
But they say it happened for me.
In a garden, on a cross, at a tomb,
It happened, for me—vicariously.
But how did it apply to me?
It was his life, not mine.
It was he who wept, who bled, who died.
In place of you and me.

The other day I was at the grocery store. I had finished my shopping and headed for the checkout counter. A young boy ahead of me in line stood at the counter with a few items to purchase. The clerk was telling him that he did not have enough money to buy everything he had, and he needed to choose something to leave behind. The poor child was terribly embarrassed.

"But this is what my mommy told me to buy. I have to get it all!" he cried. I could see the pleading in his big brown eyes, and my heart went out to this helpless lad. But the clerk remained politely firm. The boy's countenance fell, and he stood there with his chin on his chest, his face crinkled up into a tearful knot.

Then, God spoke to me. "You can help!" flooded my heart and mind. I stepped forward and pulled out my wallet. It wasn't very much that the young boy lacked. The clerk's demands were appeased; the entire debt was paid. The youngster smiled at me, mumbled his thank you, and ran happily through the electronic doors.

I had taken upon myself the debt that another could not pay. Then came my enlightenment. It was as though a still, small voice inside me spoke. All at once I understood, and was awed.

This is the same thing that had been done for me, a sinner, by the holy son of God! A price had been paid that I might "return home," freed of a great debt I was powerless to pay. There was no darkness or doubt in my mind. The tomb was empty. The price of justice had been paid. I was as the young boy at the counter, who could not pay the cost. Jesus stepped forward and paid the price I was powerless to pay.

I was not there when Jesus Christ died, but they say it happened for me. In a garden, on a cross, at a tomb . . . it happened, for me— vicariously.

—WALTER H. STEWART

*Joy is the echo of God's
life within us.*

—JOSEPH MARMION,
ORTHODOXY

Sharing the Joy

Better With Age

For more than 80 years, Mary Rose wondered what God's plan would be for her. Then she realized "that I had been doing God's work all my life."

*W*hen I first met Mary Rose, she had been living with cancer for as many years as I was old, and she boasted more replaced and "assisted" body parts than I had thought possible. She embraced every medical marvel offered —hips, knees, hearing aids, a double breast prosthesis, "store-bought teeth" (as she called them), and a motorized wheelchair—as gifts from a benevolent God who was still working on her life's plan.

Amazing.

Even more amazing was that I was interviewing her—in her nursing home room—upon the publication of her second book. The first book had debuted three years earlier, shortly after her 87th birthday.

The real story, however, was written between the lines of her poems, journals, and now her books. That story chronicled a lifetime of wait-and-see faith that had enabled her to overcome loss, her own health problems, and societal change.

"First came the horseless carriage," she told me as we turned the pages of a scrapbook. She pointed to sepia-toned photos of women in large hats drooping with veils and flowers, sitting primly on white chairs in the side yard of a church. "Then came lights, refrigeration, the vote for women, indoor plumbing, as it was delicately referred to back then. . . . I've seen two visits of Haley's Comet, men on the moon, and inventions of television and fast food, both of which I adore. Cell phones and e-mail . . . hmmm, I think not."

"There I am," she said, pointing to a photograph of a young girl in an ankle-length dress, large bow in her hair, and gloved hands holding a book. "Do you recognize it?"

I looked closer. "A Bible?"

She nodded. "This one." She picked up a worn, once-white, leather-bound Bible from the table beside her. "This is where I first learned of God's plan for me . . . the plan we're talking about today."

"You being an author?" I asked.

"I didn't know it then, of course, but yes, my books have been God's plan for me. I, on the other hand, of course, spent a lifetime looking for something else." She laughed before continuing. "Something dramatic like converting people in a foreign land, or saving lives as a medical missionary, or being a martyr for the sake of God's word." Nowadays, however, a wiser Mary Rose talks about "the simplicity of faith and its extraordinary power."

"It's taken me nearly a century to figure that out, though," she said with a quiet laugh. "But even as a child, I knew that God had a plan for me, so I just kept myself ready in the meantime."

In the meantime was marriage to the jovial, mustachioed gentleman standing beside her in wedding photographs and later together with their five children.

"I was also a bookkeeper for my husband's furniture business," she said. "It seemed so trivial, all the things I was doing. Tallying up numbers?" She shook her head. "But I tried to do it fairly and help people when I could." She hesitated before continuing. "There were a lot of people in town who got to have furniture during the Depression days at what they thought were bargains, but..."

"But?" I prompted.

"I don't mean to sound boastful, but my husband and I prayed about it and decided to have our own little 'fund' that we dipped into to help these good people." In other words, they sold furniture at prices so cheap that they took a loss. "It was the least we could do," she said.

The least? I thought to myself. It seemed like a lot to me.

Mary Rose continued. "And each day I would pray as I had done as a child: 'When, Lord, will it be my turn to do something for you?' Now, however, I began adding a small, hesitant postscript reminder: 'Remember, Lord, time is passing me by.'"

"Did you think God had forgotten you?" I asked, ready for what I was sure would be an affirmative answer.

"Why, no, dear, I just thought God might not realize how old I was getting! It never occurred to me that my turn wouldn't come or that God had no plans for me. I was more concerned about the timing. Would I be ready? Was there going to be enough room in my already busy life, especially since it already wasn't what I'd envisioned?"

It was after the great-grandchildren began to arrive that Mary Rose experienced her first doubts. Had God forgotten her?

"I had to wonder," she confessed, "how God could use an old lady."

The answer sits on many bookshelves. Fast approaching a century of life, Mary Rose became an author.

"I don't know when it was that I first realized that I had been doing God's work all my life," she said. "God had been leading me like I was on a scavenger hunt: I was guided from one small thing to another. It was God's presence that was the connecting link. Now I had something I could tell others: God uses you wherever you are."

"Even in a nursing home?" I asked.

"Especially in a nursing home," she answered in a lively voice, "for the people who are in one!"

Penned at Mary Rose's drop-leaf desk here in her small room, these small books paint a rich picture of God's constant presence and abiding wisdom. They tell how each of us can examine in our own lives, like mining for gold, those opportunities to share faith, to help those around us. As she says, "Even the smallest gesture extends God's care. . . . We are God's hands and feet."

She said about her new books: "This is just the frosting on the cake. These books are what I've been preparing for all my life. In God's time, nothing we do is wasted. He can use it somehow.

"When it was time for God to have me tie up all the loose ends I'd gathered during nearly nine decades of living, it was to write about the view I saw through my open door." She smiled and patted the book, which indeed was titled

Through My Open Door. "It seemed the perfect title. You know, you can't come here and close yourself off. Keep that door open and invite people in and venture out yourself. God might have something in mind for you down the hall."

I had already read the book before the interview and could vouch for the jacket blurb: "... a delightful tale of life in a nursing home, dispelling myths and inspiring others to take a second glance at the joys of aging." Instead of the end of the road or even a detour on a long road of steadfast faith in a practical God, Mary Rose describes how it was just another beginning.

"This is simply the next chapter in the ultimate adventure," she said with a smile.

—MARGARET ANNE HUFFMAN

Enjoying the View

Why do we sometimes fixate on the "bare trees" when God has blessed us with so much beauty?

"*I*s anyone from out of state?" the tour guide asked.

I raised my hand.

"Where are you from?"

"Florida," I said. *Where there is nothing to compare with the beauty of autumn we're seeing here,* I felt like adding.

While we waited for our afternoon tour to begin, I asked the lady next to me where she lived.

"St. Charles," she said, adding, "You know, I was here last week, and the leaves were stupendous on this tour."

"They look lovely today," I said. "And it's a perfect day."

The temperature was around 74, the sun shone brightly, and a gentle breeze rustled the leaves. I felt like a tourist who had just discovered a gold mine. Although I had passed this arboretum every day on my way to junior college years before, I had taken it all for granted back then.

As the bus started on the tour, the lady next to me said, "I notice a lot of leaves have fallen since last week. That tour was just perfect."

"That's nice," I said and turned my attention to the tour guide, who told us about Mr. Morton, the owner of the Morton Salt company, and how he had decided to build an estate here, which eventually became the Morton Arboretum.

As we rode along, the tour guide pointed out different trees. "Oohs" and "ahhs" came out of my mouth each time I turned to where she pointed.

"Look over there," the lady next to me said. "See that cluster of bare trees? Those had gorgeous red leaves on them last week. It was breathtaking."

I looked at the bare trees and tried hard not to think about what I had missed.

What about the breathtaking view on our right? I felt like asking.

"Yes, those leaves last week were so beautiful," Ms. Party Pooper rambled on. "This is nothing compared to last week."

Well, it's something for me. I haven't seen autumn leaves in years, I argued in my mind. I looked around again to see another beautiful grove of trees.

Soon we were deep in the forest. My neighbor told me again and again how the beauty of these leaves wasn't nearly as wonderful as last week. Then suddenly we were surrounded by yellow; sugar maples stretched in every direction. The tour guide stopped the bus.

"Wow! This is great," I said, enraptured by the gorgeous colors surrounding us. My neighbor was silent, but only for a moment.

"This tour guide is not as good as last week's," she whispered.

After we were out of the deep forest, the tour guide said, "On the right, you'll see the brilliant red of the bush referred to as 'the burning bush.'"

"They're not as brilliant as they were last week," my pesky neighbor added.

I wasn't here last week, so they look brilliant to me, I felt like yelling.

In the midst of my anger at this woman for wrecking my nature adventure, a gentle whisper came to my soul: *You act like her sometimes.*

As I compared the beauty of these trees to the wonder of God's love, I saw how many times I acted like this lady, keeping my mind on what God had done in the past and compar-

ing those miracles, vainly, to present negative
events—the bare trees in my life. I thought how
when I became too devoted to the pressures of
life, I no longer sensed God's presence, his
amazing love for me, and the beautiful things
he had brought into my life.

At first I felt pretty bad getting "stuck" next
to that lady. I've since concluded that maybe
she was a widow who felt she was in a "bare

trees" phase of her life. But when I think back to that day, I'm thankful for her. Through her, God showed me there will always be obstacles to sensing his love and the beauty of the world and the people around me—obstacles that come both from within and from outside myself.

Today I choose to look beyond bare trees and see the beauty all around me.

—ELAINE CREASMAN

*T*ake my yoke upon you, and learn from me; for I am gentle and humble in heart, and you will find rest for your souls. For my yoke is easy, and my burden is light.

—MATTHEW 11:29-30

The Faith Hall of Fame

Not even Babe Ruth and Joe Namath could match the heroics of Daniel, Joshua, and Moses—men who performed the ultimate acts of bravery because of their unrelenting faith in God.

"*P*apa, tell me the greatest story you know," my granddaughter requested.

My mind started reeling.

Was it the Babe? Surely no one could top the Sultan of Swat's great feat of stepping out of the batter's box and pointing to where he was going to hit a home run—and then delivering. Babe Ruth . . . the greatest.

Was it Joe Willie Namath? Telling the world that his New York Jets would whip the mighty Baltimore Colts in Super Bowl III? Then he went out and led his team to victory on two bum knees.

Was it Kip Keino, the great African runner who ran the Olympic marathon race—all 26 miles of it—barefoot?

I looked down at my Sweet Pea, her big blue eyes dancing with excitement and anticipation, when I realized I was in the wrong arena, looking at the wrong game. Granted, these were great stories, but Sweet Pea asked for the greatest story—my best shot.

A warm glow came over me as I turned to her and said, "Sweet Pea, do you know what faith is?"

She shook her head no, so I asked her, "What do you do when we're down in the basement and you see a cricket?"

"I jump into your arms!" she said as she leapt onto me.

"And what did I just do?" I asked as she nestled in my arms.

"You caught me, Papa."

"How did you know I was going to catch you?"

"'Cause I'm your Sweet Pea and you always catch me," she replied with a smile that could melt an iceberg.

"So, you had faith that I would catch you and protect you from that cricket, right?"

"Right!" she said.

"Sweet Pea, ever hear of Daniel?"

"Who?"

I shared the story of Daniel with her.

"Daniel kneeled before his God, knowing the law of the land would condemn him to the lion's den. Daniel could have easily worshiped behind closed doors and avoided certain death. No one would have known. Instead, he chose to be seen. He chose the lion's den. Top that one— the Babe Ruth of faith stories."

"Tell me an even bigger story, Papa!" my Sweet Pea demanded.

"Okay, how 'bout the big three: Shadrach, Meshach, and Abednego? Like Daniel, they knew beforehand what the consequences of their actions would be—in their case, a fiery furnace if they did not fall down and worship Nebuchanezzar's golden image. Like Daniel, they could have gone through the motions of 'faking it' with the idol—making it look good and avoiding the hot seat. They chose the furnace! Can you imagine the faith it took, the feelings they must have experienced as the door to the furnace was opened?"

"Tell me more!" she cried. "Even bigger, Papa!"

"How 'bout David as he walked out to face Goliath? Or Joshua as he presented to his people what had to sound like the craziest plans to capture Jericho? They marched around the walls of the city in silence for six days, and on the seventh day they marched around the city seven times, and..."

"They did what?"

"They did exactly what God had told them to do. They marched around the city for six days in silence, and on the seventh day they marched around the city seven times. And then, the seven priests blew their trumpets, and the people shouted as they were told to do, and guess what happened?"

"What?"

"The walls of Jericho came tumbling down."

"They had great faith, huh, Papa?"

"Great faith, Sweet Pea. Great faith."

"Tell me more, Papa. Tell me another great story of faith."

"How about Moses? So many times he displayed the faith of champions—from refusing to be called the son of Pharaoh's daughter to passing through the Red Sea...now there's a sight for you! The ultimate sacrifice of faith, you ask? How about Abraham's willingness to sacrifice his only son, Isaac. And don't forget the most ridiculed and mocked for his faith: old Noah, as he built the ark."

On and on the stories of great faith abound, like the centurion who told Jesus: "Don't bother wasting your time coming to my house. It is not worthy of your presence. Your word is all I need.... Just say the word and I'll know my servant is healed." What a beautiful story of faith.

Sweet Pea heard them all.

The Faith Hall of Fame.

Where legends abound.

The same faith we have access to.

The same God.

Sorry, Babe and Joe Willie.

You're out of your league on this one.

—JOE PRITCHARD

Painting the Truth

As with a great painting, perspective and light help us to fully experience the grace of God.

I wanted to reach into my canvas and straighten the barn I'd made crooked with paint. The road in the painting wasn't right, either. It seemed to jet skyward rather than snake gracefully over the hill toward the meadow as it did in my intention.

As I waited for my critique with the art teacher, I thought of what had prodded me back into painting after two nonproductive years. I'd reached a disappointing plateau in my artwork and had no desire to continue at that mediocre level.

Then, at a seminar on Christianity and the Arts, the speaker had said, "It is an artist's responsibility to paint the truth." It seemed a worthy goal, and my desire to paint was rekindled. Now, in class with the muddled mess before me, I wondered if I would ever learn to "paint the truth."

The teacher, with her experienced eye, quickly evaluated my morning's work.

"The barn is kitty wumpus (her pet words for crooked)," she said, "and your road isn't in perspective."

With a deft touch of the brush, she shored up the barn and laid the road to rest on the contour of the hill. All the time she worked, she spoke of perspective.

"You need to make all lines and angles conform to the law of perspective," she said. Glancing around the room, she noticed other students struggling with "kitty wumpus" buildings. She had us put down our brushes and pick up our pens to take notes on the principles of perspective.

Over the next few weeks, while I struggled with the truth of what she'd said, my teacher painted me out of trouble time and again.

One day, when I was painting at home alone, my boats looked like bananas—and there was no one to bail me out this time. I turned to my notebook and found the principles of perspective. So *that* was it! I had forgotten one important point that helped everything make sense.

As I applied paint with the basic point in mind, the newly aligned boats appeared seaworthy.

It's like life, I thought. When I neglect to line up my life by God's perspective, to pray and study the word even for a day, my life gets "kitty wumpus." Human emotions, human opinion replace God's truth. I shuttered to think how many times, how many ways I may have led others on crooked paths of human error, how many times I missed God's best for me by not being lined up with truth.

With new resolve, I became determined to make the words in Colossians 2:6–8 a personal experience: "As you therefore have received Christ Jesus the Lord, continue to live your lives in him, rooted and built up in him and established in the faith, just as you were taught,

abounding in thanksgiving. See to it that no
one takes you captive through philosophy and
empty deceit, according to human tradition,
according to the elemental spirits of the universe, and not according to Christ."

I was glad for the insight, but there was
more the Lord would teach me about truth
through painting.

After I learned to paint sturdy buildings,
float able boats, and construct roads that led
somewhere, I was content . . . for a while. Something was lacking. My work was technically
correct, but boring.

"What does it need?" I lamented to my
teacher.

The trained eye knew. "Sunshine," she
offered. "Hit the sunlit places with reflective
light. That will make your painting sing!"

I picked up a large brush, loaded it with
sunshine, and splashed yellow and golds on
every surface.

"Overdone," the teacher critiqued.

"How do you know where to put the sunlight?" I sighed, wondering if I would *ever*
create an acceptable painting—that told the
truth.

"Only the objects that have nothing
between them and the sun will reflect the

light." My teacher moved on to the next student, leaving me to determine which patches of sunshine were genuine and which, because they didn't come from the true source, weren't real and couldn't remain.

Hmmm, I pondered. The shack on the pier is in the sunlight, as is one of the boats. The blue rowboat can't be reflective, though; it's in the shadow of the dock.

My brush flitted across the canvas, dabbing here, dabbing there, lifting the sunshine that wasn't real. As I wiped a glob of misplaced sunshine from my brush with a paper towel, it triggered a memory of a man I had read about. He had said, "I'm tired of pretending to be happy and on top of things all the time. I'm not." And his self-generated sparkle burned out.

I hope that one of the Lord's reflective people lit the darkness for that man. From 2 Corinthians 4:6: "For it is the God who said, 'Let light shine out of darkness,' who has shone in our hearts to give the light of the knowledge of the glory of God in the face of Jesus Christ."

I saw with new clarity the necessity of having nothing between myself and God's son if I were to reflect his light.

I stepped away from the easel for a long view and backed into another painter, who was also moving away from her picture.

"Sorry," we both said at once. She turned to look at my work.

"You've really captured the sunlight," she said. "It's like the teacher says: 'It sings!'"

"Thanks," I said, enjoying the encouragement, but I wanted to hear it from the teacher. Before that would happen, my painted medley was to include another tone—in a minor key.

The teacher frowned when she stepped up to my easel. Her knowing eyes darted from one area of the canvas to another. And then she turned the painting upside down and continued to scrutinize. *What on earth is she looking for?* I wondered. *Is my painting so bad that she couldn't tell it was right-side up?* I busied myself by cleaning paint off my hands while she continued to study the piece.

My hands were free of paint and I was dabbing at my forearm before she spoke. "Your painting is quite good," she said. "In fact, some might consider it finished. But I am interested in turning a good painting into an excellent one. By turning it upside down, I'm not distracted by each component, but I see the overall effect—the balance of all the parts. What your

painting needs is depth. You accomplish that with dark areas and shadows."

She picked up my palette knife and poked spikes of warm color into the darkest paint pools on the mixing pad.

"These tones will bring vibrancy into your dark areas," she said. "At first glance, your rocks might appear to be solid black, but a closer look will reveal that they're not. And shadows aren't all gray, you know. Come here." She led me toward the window. "Look out there and squint your eyes while you look at the shadows from the trees. What do you notice?"

I narrowed my eyes and concentrated on the crisscrossing shadows gracing the snow. "Why, they're beautiful!" I exclaimed. "There's a variety of shades in them, and they seem to flow with the lay of the land."

I sauntered back toward my easel, absorbed in my new discovery.

"Here," the teacher said, handing me the paint-loaded knife, "make that painting make a statement!"

I stood there looking at the dark but lively paint on the knife—and at the sunlit scene that moments before had seemed so satisfactory. Would darkness and shadows *really* enhance the picture?

Quickly, with quick, staccato motions, I cut the mellowing colors into the black rocks and the water that swirled around them—blue, turquoise, purple, green. All over the canvas I intruded with stabs and drags of dark swipes. It seemed harsh, but I kept imposing the sobering tones. The teacher had said to do it, and I trusted her judgment. And then she was at my elbow.

"Step across the room," she said, "and see your work from a different perspective."

Crossing the room, I wondered what she would point out this time. I turned toward the painting. A joyous harmony emanated from the canvas. The dark areas and shadows that I had resisted and feared brought balance and depth. The sunlit places radiated a compelling warmth.

Out of the painted shadows came another glimmer of truth for me to treasure and learn to grow from.

In my life, if I had my choice, I'd opt for all sunshine—continuous joy, a sense of God's presence, never-ending peace, victory, success—and no pain or problems. But the Master Artist uses the trials that send us to our knees. They keep us close to him, develop our sensitivity to others, enlarge our vision, stretch us, and help us grow toward wholeness.

A balanced painting is a constant reminder of God's grace. When I sense that I've gone "kitty wumpus" and have lost my spiritual perspective, a glance at the painting reminds me that I need to go to the word and refocus my sights. When I get irritable and unloving, the objects in shadow make me aware that my light has dimmed because I've stepped out of the Son shine.

—PRISCILLA LARSON

Eyes Wide Open

**We can't see God, but we know he's with us—
or at least in the other room!**

My children's Sunday school class always began with prayer. We'd sit in a circle on the floor, the little ones all following my lead as I bowed my head and closed my eyes. Only my eyes would pop open again to make sure everyone behaved. But this one morning, a small boy, Chad, kept his eyes wide open and watched me intently as I prayed.

When the prayer ended, he announced, "You prayed just like God was right here in the room with us."

"Yes," I explained. "That's right. He's right here."

The child looked around and frowned, as if in search of God, clearly not understanding. The harder I tried to explain, the more baffled he became. I kept trying to tell him that God was always there, though we couldn't see him, that it was faith to believe in God when we couldn't actually see him. I told the children that it was like the air in the room, always there even though we couldn't see it. No, that didn't help. How could I explain such a difficult idea to such young children? Even adults grappled with this one at times, how to know God was present when he couldn't be seen.

After struggling for words he could grasp, I suddenly felt a flash of pure inspiration. Surely this was straight from God, a perfect way to show the children what I meant.

"Go out to the hall," I instructed the youngster, feeling immensely pleased with myself. Once he was out in the hall, out of our sight, I explained to everyone that this was faith, that we knew Chad was still there even though we couldn't see him. The children seemed to understand this much better than any of my other attempts.

"Come on back in the room, Chad," I called. "See," I told him. "You were out of the room. We couldn't see you, but we all still knew you were there. Do you see what I mean? God is always here even though we can't see him. That's what faith is."

I felt wonderful. All the lights blazed in that small child's eyes. He finally understood. That's when teaching swelled my heart with joy, when a small child understood a spiritual truth. I felt great the rest of the day. I'd solved a difficult problem with skill and grace.

My smug sense of what a fine teacher I was collapsed, though, when later Chad's parents told me how he'd explained what he'd learned in class that day.

"See, Mom," he had said, grinning. "Faith is knowing that whenever God goes out in the hall at church on Sundays, we can be sure he'll always be right back!"

—Karen M. Leet

The Power of Faith

*F*aith makes all evil good to us, and all good better; unbelief makes all good evil, and all evil worse. Faith laughs at the shaking of the spear; unbelief trembles at the shaking of a leaf, unbelief starves the soul; faith finds food in famine, and a table in the wilderness. In the greatest danger, faith said, "I have a great God." When outward strength is broken, faith rests on the promises. In the midst of sorrow, faith draws the sting out of every trouble, and takes out the bitterness from every affliction.

—ROBERT CECIL (1563–1612)

A Change of Heart

Changing your habits can change your attitude—and your life.

*Y*ou know, I am not an educated woman, but I have learned this much: It's far easier to change habits than it is to change attitudes. If I wait for my attitude to change before I overhaul sinful behavior, it never happens. But if I change my actions, despite my human inclinations, I develop a new habit, and eventually my attitude follows.

For years I struggled with pent-up anger. As long as I can remember, it was a lifelong preoccupation. I nurtured anger toward parents, my sister, my schoolmates, my cousins. I could recite dialogue word for word to myself: "And then she said . . . and then I said . . . and then she said." Ad nauseam. It kept me occupied in the dentist's chair, in the backseat of the car, during study hall, during sermons, and through many sleepless nights.

As I grew older, I was still brooding over events that had occurred 20 years earlier, inventing better retorts, imagining the offender eating crow, or finding ways to heap guilt upon them for hurting me. I would wash the dishes and find everything cleaned up and put away, without having given one thought to the chore because I was so totally carried away in a memory fraught with anger, hurt, and imagined vengeance.

The truth is, I reveled in these flights of fury.

Shortly after I turned 40, I became seriously ill. In a moment of spiritual clarity in my hospital bed, God spoke to me. It was the "still, small voice" kind of experience. It dawned on me that perhaps the playing and replaying of these toxic "tapes" had contributed to my health problems. So I devised a plan to change my heart and my habits—and hopefully my health.

The plan was this: The very moment I recognized that I was off on an inner rage, I would interrupt myself and start to recite Bible verses. If I finished the scripture and went right back to where I left off, I moved on to singing hymns. I'd do it out loud, no matter where I was. I got really good at memorizing the first stanza of all the hymns in the Methodist hymnal.

One moment I'd be clenching my teeth, lamenting some hurtful event, and the next I'd be belting out "Amazing Grace." (Eventually, I learned all of the verses of that song.) Cab drivers looked at me nervously through the rearview mirror. Strangers on the street smiled—or crossed over to the other side of the street. Even the people at work got used to hearing one song or another winging out of my office. (Did I mention that I have a terrible voice?)

One of my favorite hymns was written by Horatio Spafford, a successful Chicago lawyer, who, in 1873, lost four daughters in a ship-wreck. From his grief, he penned the words to the only hymn he ever wrote, "It Is Well With My Soul." The first stanza, which I of course memorized, reads:

When peace, like a river, attendenth my way,
When sorrows like sea billows roll;
Whatever my lot, thou hast taught me to say,
It is well, it is well with my soul.

Clearly, God wanted me to change, and the difference in my life is immeasurable. Yes, I have recovered from my illness. And I have discovered a great deal of peace. Yet at times I still feel incredible sorrow over the real and imagined pains that immobilized my life for too long. Fortunately, the number of times I need to burst into song has dwindled. And I have come to appreciate the recall I have of so many Bible verses. But *finally* I can sing with dear Mr. Spafford: "It is well, it is well with my soul."

—SHARYN VARGO

What Goes Around Comes Around

What better way to share your joy than
through a vanity license plate?

*A*fter enduring nine-hour back surgery in
1990, and because I suffer from degener-
ative osteoarthritis, I am now handicapped.
Throughout my life, but especially since that
surgery, I've been the recipient of countless acts
of kindness by friends and strangers alike. I
wished there was a way for me to show my
appreciation to the world at large, and to say
thank you from deep in my heart to the many
people who have helped me.

I decided to get vanity license plates for my
car, and I searched for an appropriate message.
I thought of nicknames, initials, numbers of
grandchildren, and other meaningful short
words, but nothing seemed quite right.

Then lightning struck! The thought
popped into my head, and I knew right away it
would be perfect: "BLESSU!" I ordered the
plates and anxiously awaited their arrival.

Great has been the reward of sharing the
joy that abounds in my heart via my license

plates. A stranger waiting by my car in zero-degree weather asked me to pray for her husband, who was having brain surgery. A motorist pulled up next to me at a red light,

motioned for me to roll down my window, and said, "I like your license plate, and bless you, too!" This incident was especially meaningful, since my daughter and I were on our way to the hospital, where I was to have thyroid surgery several hours later. It was like a message from on high that brought peace and joy to my heart.

Each time my car is serviced at the garage and my license plate letters are recorded on the worksheet, I see the BLESSU written by someone else. At such times, amazingly and unwittingly I, too, become the recipient!

You see, what goes around comes around!

—LORRAYNE E. HOCKMAN

*He that giveth unto the poor
shall not lack.*

—Proverbs 28:27 (KJV)

Give and You
Shall Receive

The Gift

A mother of four gave every dollar in her pocket to her church—only to be rewarded in ways far greater than money.

*S*ales had been extremely slow in our family business, and my husband and I were struggling to pay our bills. With four children and a mortgage, we were desperate. At night as my husband, Fred, snored, the smell of stale beer filling our bedroom, I would turn away from him and pray silently for God's help.

It was unusually warm that Wednesday night as I walked into my church for evening services, but I felt compelled to go directly to the altar. It would be at least 30 minutes before services would begin, and I was glad to be able to spend the time in prayer.

Usually I sit up front, where I can hear and see everything, but that night as I rose from the altar I noticed that we had an unusually large crowd, forcing me to sit in the back. Chalking it up to my run of bad luck, and not our esteemed guest speaker, I settled into the farthest pew.

I struggled to hear the sermon above the noise of restless children and window fans. Our district missionary was speaking about overcoming the language barriers in New Guinea, and my mind kept wandering off. I had exactly $50 in my pocket—money that was supposed to go toward our groceries. But I felt an overwhelming urge to put it in the offering. All of it. It had been a subtle nag at first, which I tried to ignore. It became so strong, though, that it could not be denied.

A few resonant notes from the organ signaled that it was time for the offering. I shifted in my seat and watched as the shiny gold plates passed silently from person to person. When the deacon passed the plate to my pew, I felt myself pull that money out of my pocket and slip it in. For a second I held onto the plate, wanting to grab the money back. My husband was going to be so angry with me. Then, as I passed the plate to my neighbor, a feeling of peace came over me. Somehow I knew that the Lord would take care of it.

I was right on both counts. My husband was very angry. The next three days were thoroughly unpleasant. On the afternoon of the third day, I went to get our mail, dreading all the bills I knew would be there. As I sorted through them, I found an envelope that I didn't recognize. Of course, I tore it open first. To my surprise there was a check for over $400—more than enough for groceries and some past-due bills.

That evening as I prayed, I thought about my plea that Wednesday night at the altar. I had begged the Lord to help us. His answer, I realized, was on its way before I had even asked.

God's work really is perfect. Had it been the regular Wednesday night service, I would have been sitting up front, totally engrossed in the sermon. But that night I was forced to sit in the back, where I had a hard time hearing. He wanted my full attention and he wanted me to take one small step of faith.

From that experience, I learned that my life truly is in God's hands. But even better, it got the notice of my husband. Fred now believes in God and knows that he cares about us. Today we attend church together, and even more miraculously Fred is always right there when he hears of others who are in need.

I know that the money would have come to us anyway. God doesn't ask us to give so that we can get rich. He asked me to trust him so that he could teach me about faith—and so that he might capture my husband's full attention. It was all part of his marvelous plan.

Although that night when I left the church I felt as if I had gotten absolutely nothing out of the service, I learned days later that I had indeed received a great gift—a gift so great that its richness will shine forever.

—SHERRY MARTIN

A Coincidence?

"Give, and it will be given to you. A good
measure, pressed down, shaken together and
running over, will be poured into your lap.
For with the measure you use,
it will be measured to you."
Luke 6:38 (NIV)

I was very proud of my daughter Emily. At
only nine years old, she had been carefully
saving her allowance money all year and trying
to earn extra money by doing small jobs
around the neighborhood. Emily was determined to save enough to buy a girl's mountain
bike, an item for which she'd been longing, and
she'd been faithfully putting her money away
since the beginning of the year.

"How are you doing, honey?" I asked soon
after Thanksgiving. I knew she had hoped to
have all the money she needed by the end of the
year.

"I have 49 dollars, Daddy," she said. "I'm
not sure if I'm going to make it."

"You've worked so hard," I said encouragingly. "Keep it up. But you know that you can
have your pick from my bicycle collection."

"Thanks, Daddy. But your bikes are so *old.*"

I smiled to myself because I knew she was right. As a collector of vintage bicycles, all my girl's bikes were 1950s models—not the kind a kid would choose today.

When the Christmas season arrived, Emily and I went comparison shopping, and she saw several less expensive bikes for which she thought she'd have to settle. As we left one store, she noticed a Salvation Army volunteer ringing his bell by a big kettle. "Can we give them something, Daddy?" she asked.

"Sorry, Em, I'm out of change," I replied.

Emily continued to work hard all through December, and it seemed she might make her goal after all. Then suddenly one day, she came downstairs to the kitchen and made an announcement to her mother.

"Mom," she said hesitantly, "you know all the money I've been saving?"

"Yes, dear," smiled my wife, Diane.

"God told me to give it to the poor people."

Diane knelt down to Emily's level. "That's a very kind thought, sweetheart. But you've been saving all year. Maybe you could give *some* of it."

Emily shook her head vigorously. "God said *all.*"

When we saw she was serious, we gave her various suggestions about where she could contribute. But Emily had received specific instructions, and so one cold Sunday morning before Christmas, with little fanfare, she handed her total savings of $58 to a surprised and grateful Salvation Army volunteer.

Moved by Emily's selflessness, I suddenly noticed that a local car dealer was collecting used bicycles to refurbish and give to poor people for Christmas. And I realized that if my nine-year-old daughter could give away all her money, I could certainly give up one bike from my collection.

As I picked up a shiny but old-fashioned kid's bike from the line in the garage, it seemed as if a second bicycle in the line took on a glow. Should I give a *second* bike? No, certainly the one would be enough.

But as I got to my car, I couldn't shake the feeling that I should donate that second bike as well. And if Emily could follow heavenly instructions, I decided I could, too. I turned back and loaded the second bike into the trunk, then took off for the dealership.

When I delivered the bikes, the car dealer thanked me and said, "You're making two kids very happy, Mr. Koper. And here are your tickets."

"Tickets?" I asked.

"Yes. For each bike donated, we're giving away one chance to win a brand-new men's 21-speed mountain bike from a local bike shop. So here are your tickets for two chances."

Why wasn't I surprised when that second ticket won the bike? "I can't believe you won!" laughed Diane, delighted.

"I didn't," I said. "It's pretty clear that Emily did."

And why wasn't I surprised when the bike dealer happily substituted a gorgeous new girl's mountain bike for the man's bike advertised?

Coincidence? Maybe. I like to think it was God's way of rewarding a little girl for a sacrifice beyond her years—while giving her dad a lesson in charity and the power of the Lord.

—Ed Koper ©

*T*ruly I tell you, if you have faith the size of a mustard seed, you will say to this mountain, "Move from here to there," and it will move; and nothing will be impossible for you.

—Matthew 17:20

One Tract

Jenny decided to spread the Good News, not realizing it would take off like wildfire.

"*W*ait a minute," Jenny called to her neighbor, feeling a strong urge to run back inside and snatch up a gospel tract. "Here, take this, OK?"

Then they hugged goodbye, and her neighbor, Laura, set off on her first vacation in five years. She intended to enjoy every single moment. Even boarding the plane was pure joy.

She and her seatmate hit it off instantly, chatting easily, getting to know each other, becoming almost friends during their flight. Shortly before landing, Laura reached in her purse to find mints and discovered the scripture booklet Jenny had felt that strong urge to give her. Pulling it out, she leafed through it, and her seatmate noticed.

"What's that?" she asked, so Laura passed it right along. Who knew? Maybe this was the reason Jenny had given it to her. The seatmate looked it over casually, then tucked it inside her own purse as they left the plane. They went

their separate ways, the seatmate glad to be
done with her business trip and safely home
again.

Once home, she slid back into routine and
forgot the tract, only finding it when she emptied her purse onto the table to hunt for a
misplaced store receipt. Her husband found it
there and picked it up to glance through it.

"Hey," he told her, "this looks like something my sister might like to take a look at. OK
with you if I send it to her?" And so he did,
right in the next day's mail.

His sister read it over, liking the look of it,
and showed it to her closest friend, who looked
it over and left it on the coffee table—where her
father happened to see it. He picked it up,
leafed through it, and got to thinking. His
buddy at work might take a look at this booklet. It was brightly colored, interesting, and
crammed full of truth. So, he took it along to

work and handed it to his friend, who read it carefully, drawn somehow to the bright cover and the words inside.

The more he read, the more he was moved and touched and pulled by the words inside. The message gripped him and wouldn't let go. And at last he bowed his head, prayed, and believed. He could scarcely wait to call his daughter to tell her the news. Hadn't she prayed for him all these years?

"Hello," he said. "Jenny..."

—KAREN M. LEET

*I*t is never a question with
any of us of faith or no faith;
the question always is, "In
what or in whom do we
put our faith?"

—ANONYMOUS

The Three Trees
An American Folktale

Three little trees stood high upon a mountain discussing their dreams for the future. The first little tree looked up at the dazzling night sky and said, "I want to carry the treasure of kings and queens. I want to be beautiful. I want to be filled with all the riches in the world."

The nearby stream caught the second little tree's eye. "I want to be a mighty sailing vessel," he said. "I want to sail in the roaring oceans, roam the high seas, and deliver kings and queens safely to their destinations."

The third little tree loved the mountaintop. "I want to stay right here and grow and grow and grow," she said. "I want the people that pass by to look at me touching heaven and think of God."

One day, many years later, three powerful lumberjacks came to help the three trees with the next season of their lives.

The first tree, now stunningly beautiful, was cut down. "I will become the most beautiful treasure chest," he thought. "I will get to hold all of the world's riches."

The mighty second tree was cut down. "I will now sail the roaring oceans," thought the second tree. "I will be the mightiest of all sailing vessels."

The third tree, with her branches stretched toward heaven, was also cut down. Together with the other two trees, she was taken down the lovely hillside.

The first tree arrived at a carpenter's shop. The beautiful tree was aglow with excitement. But he wasn't made into a treasure chest. The skillful carpenter made the beautiful tree into an ordinary feeding trough.

The second tree was brought to a shipyard. The mighty second tree thought, "Now I will be the most vigorous of vessels." But the strong second tree was made into a simple little fishing boat.

The third tree was brought to a lumberyard. There she was made into beams and put aside. "Why did this happen?" thought the third tree. "All I ever wanted was to touch heaven."

As the weeks passed, their dreams began to fade from memory. However, one magical night brought the first tree's dream to life. A young mother put her newborn into the trough. "This manger is perfect," said the mother to her husband. And the first tree knew he was cradling the most important treasure ever.

One night the fishing boat was used by a tired traveler and his friends. They quickly fell asleep, and the small boat floated out to sea. The sea became rough, and a thunderstorm was brewing. This frightened the second tree. If only he were a mighty vessel and could withstand the force of the storm! The traveler was awakened by the storm, and he stretched out his arms and said, "Peace." The sea became calm and the thunderstorm vanished. It was then that the second tree realized he was carrying the Almighty King.

On a Friday morning, the third tree was taken by soldiers and carried through a hostile mob. She trembled with fear and distaste as a man's hands were nailed to her. But the following Sunday the sun rose. The earth was full of joy. She realized that everything had changed because of God's love.

The first tree was made beautiful.

The second tree was made mighty.

The third tree made people think of God.

Now faith is the assurance of things hoped for, the conviction of things not seen.

—Hebrews 11:1

Come to me,
all you that are weary and are
carrying heavy burdens, and
I will give you rest.

—MATTHEW 11:28

God's Soothing Hand

Second Time Around the Rosie

Suddenly responsible for three grandchildren,
Sarajean teamed up with God to meet the
challenge.

*I*t was the call every parent dreads: "There's
been an accident."

Sarajean's slowed-down middle years and
casual retirement vanished in the ringing of the
telephone.

She sat at the funeral of her beloved son
and daughter-in-law with a grandchild on
either side of her and another one cradled on
her lap. The preacher talked, friends eulogized,
and family members wept. All the while, Sarajean felt a shaking of her faith.

"However," she said softly to herself as the
final hymn drew the congregation to its feet.
However. There was no need to continue even if
she could have swallowed around the tears
enough to speak, for she knew that God would
finish the sentence. It had happened so many
times before, she had lost count.

Times of change, illness, financial stresses,
her late husband's final illness. . . . God had
always been there.

But now? This? She allowed herself to wonder.

It would give anyone pause, she thought. Yet despite her worries, of one thing she was certain: In times of trouble, faith is an energy source, urging us to "hold on, hold on" as God works his amazing plan in each of our lives. She also knew that the God who had brought these precious grandchildren into her life at their births was not one to stand idly by now that they were moving into her home and life and deeper into her heart.

In that assurance, she scooped up the two youngest children, one in each arm, and instructed the oldest child to hold onto her dress as she led them from the church and on to the cemetery. And then, from there, ready or not, they would enter a new world—a world they would all have to piece together, like the quilts Sarajean often made.

Ball games, potty training, Santa Claus, training wheels, Tooth Fairy, parent-teacher conferences. Sarajean had been there, done that, but faced doing it again. Three times. It was a new role—although not a repeat performance, she was surprised to discover. It was a different world into which these children were drawing her.

"Raising these three is both joy and pain," Sarajean explained frankly when her friends asked her how she was doing. "Sometimes I think about what I would be doing if I weren't planning for spring break, buying school clothes, keeping up with the latest toys and games, and I feel overwhelmed, sad, frustrated. Loving them is not the issue. It's just that my life is so different from what I thought it would be by now.

"It's obviously what I'm supposed to be doing," she said, just a trifle wistfully. For nowadays, instead of fishing the lakes and roaming the country in her new mobile home, Sarajean sold the vehicle to pay for two new sewing machines and an assistant to help make quilts. Children, as she was often overheard saying, still could eat you out of house and home.

When not piecing together her lovely quilts, she was gathering the mismatched moments of childhood left in her care. She loyally provided attendance at school programs, tucking in at night, birthday cakes, family vacations, and whatever else was needed for grandchildren who missed their mother and father.

It was all worth it when the oldest, and hardest hit, said one night after prayers, "Mammaw, I love you more than the whole universe."

It was a universe, however, that needed constant explanation about why it didn't include Mom and Dad. One day, the youngest, then in second grade, brought home a family portrait she had drawn as a classroom project. In the foreground was a house, trees, flowers, a grandmother quilting, Petunia the dog, two yellow cats, and three children.

"My Family," was the caption. Up in one corner of the picture was a small, square inset with faces of a man and a woman. An arrow pointed to them with the carefully printed postscript, "Mommy and Daddy in Heaven."

Sarajean felt quiet satisfaction: She and God must be doing OK in their partnership if the child had such a wonderful understanding of both the sad reality and the vigorous, faith-filled hope of their lives.

"But, dear God," she prayed in a quiet moment as she faced the monitor of a PC, "I'm too old to learn how to work a computer. Can you teach even this old dog new tricks?" The children needed it for school, and she'd vowed she would never let them fall behind because of her.

"You may seem to be an 'old dog' to your-self," came her answer. "However, to me you are still an adventurer. Let's boot this thing up!"

God provided lots of other moments of laughter as Sarajean stretched her limits: play-ing an impromptu game of football by moon-light, learning the rosters of baseball and football teams, acquiring a taste for anchovies on pizza, and, most amazingly, discovering she actually liked music played loudly.

The bottom line, she reported with glee, was that it was fun!

In a gesture of what Sarajean knew was grace, God also filled her with a serenity and wisdom she had not had while raising her own children. If schedules and baths, for instance, got out of whack once in awhile, she knew that the children wouldn't suffer. And sometimes, especially on the anniversary of their parents' deaths, she let them all play hooky from school and go on a special outing instead. Once school officials heard her explanation, they—unofficially, of course—turned a blind eye.

Sarajean organized a support group for other grandparents raising grandkids and learned she was far from alone. It was also a good source for fellow quilters, and she needed extra hands since she'd started donating many of them to the local youth shelter. Without her, that's where her grandchildren would've wound up.

"However," God had said. "However old or tired or worried you are, we'll do this together."

"Through the years, my faith just keeps growing stronger," she explained to her new friends, "not because worries and responsibilities have eased, but because there's always that assurance that God will finish my sentence. All I have to do is explain my problem, and God says, 'Yes, I understand. However . . .' And then I can just keep going." She looked at her watch.

"Like right now," she said, jumping to her feet. "I'm off to the high school. The middle child is swimming in her first meet. I'm helping with the scoring. I didn't even know you kept score for swimming. However, God willing, I'll keep learning this and whatever else it takes."

—MARGARET ANNE HUFFMAN

Remembering What Matters

Sometimes we need the Lord's strong hand to pull us out of bed.

*T*here are days when it's best to just stay in bed. When those kind of days extend into weeks and then into months... well, it's not easy to get out of bed at all. I should know. For a month I was one with the dust ruffle. The following month I definitely bonded with my bed. It's almost three months, and I'm just now able to throw back the covers. I suspect I'll get up enough nerve to look for my robe and slippers soon.

It began a while ago. My four-wheel-drive vehicle had been out of warranty for 37 days when it started making a metal-on-metal scraping sound. A day later it began vibrating. At stoplights it sounded like a dragster. Then, leaving work late that night, I realized my headlights were not as bright as usual. The right headlight had burned out. Although I was helpless to deal with the engine problems, replacing a headlamp was surely within my limited mechanical repertoire. How hard could it be to go to the local auto parts store, buy a replacement bulb, and install it?

The most brilliant engineers in America guaranteed my failure.

My headlight was located behind the battery, under several coolant hoses, and just out of reach of the human hand. Undaunted, I removed the battery (which triggered the car alarm and erased all of the data stored in the onboard computer), wiggled my now skinless hand between coolant hoses, and ripped the entire headlamp from its plastic mount! I'm quite sure I saw the service manager snicker as he handed me the repair bill. No scraping sounds, a smooth ride, and a new headlight—all for $1,287.54.

I'd taught adult education classes for about five years in our church when they asked me to take on our youth ministry. I never thought I had much to say to teenagers, or knew what it took to connect with them. But I soon found that they, like everyone else, just needed to know God's love. So my wife, Chris, and I started loving them and teaching them, and the group began to grow and grow.

Then one Sunday the deacons asked us to meet with them after the service. The meeting did not go well. The church was without a pastor, and they thought we would better serve the church by teaching an adult class again. The discussion heated up. We felt committed to the kids. The deacons thought we should be shepherding the adults. Bottom line: They asked us to step down and let a younger couple take over. We were devastated, and the kids felt abandoned by us. So I went to bed.

One morning Chris deftly pushed an envelope under the quilt. It was a letter I had been waiting for. She was sure *this* would snatch me out from under the sheets. I ripped open the envelope and unfolded the pages. In the seven years since I started my own business, I had prayed for the opportunity to bid on a really big job. When I finally got the chance, I knew it could be the job of a lifetime. It would keep me and my employees busy for several months, provide well for Chris and me, and give my business some much-needed visibility in our community. I had worked hard for this opportunity, and the fact that they asked me to submit a proposal at all reflected some regard for my firm. Despite what had happened at church, at least my career was finally going to get the recognition it deserved.

Perhaps bad things really do occur in threes. I stared at the pages, rereading each one several times. As good as my price was, I had been underbid by a significant amount. The job had gone to someone else. I was sure there had been a mistake. There wasn't.

By now the bed is comparable to a small trailer home. *My* small trailer home.

It's hard to describe how low I felt: paying a car repair bill that I couldn't afford, losing the bonds we'd built with the church kids, then watching the job of a lifetime go to someone less competent. Combined, they sent me into a fog of self-pity and depression that I couldn't escape.

Not only is the bed my new home, but I am pretty sure I'll need to install a shower in the coming weeks.

Then, like a tiny bit of static electricity, it hit me. A fleeting thought about God and his omnipotence cracked my consciousness. I went back to sleep, but I awoke to a flood of such thoughts. He is in charge of everything, and nothing happens without his knowledge and stamp of approval. All things work together for good to those who love him. Suddenly, I remembered that I was *loved*. I smiled again for the first time in a long time. And thus I began the process of getting out of bed and finding my robe and *slippers!*

—Tom Rhodes

EDITOR'S NOTE: GOD LED CHRIS AND TOM TO A
NEW CHURCH FAMILY, WHERE THEY'VE BECOME
INVOLVED IN THE STUDENT MINISTRY.
THEIR BUSINESS COMPETITOR IS STILL WORKING
ON THE JOB HE UNDERBID, AND MANY OF HIS
REGULAR CLIENTS HAVE HIRED TOM TO
TAKE ON THEIR CURRENT PROJECTS....
AND TOM'S KNUCKLES ARE HEALING NICELY.

Scrap Heap Heart

One day Darcy realized that she relied too much on her husband—and not enough on the Lord.

*D*id you ever fall head over heels in love with someone? There's no other feeling quite like it. The sun always seems to shine, and even thunderclouds have a gleaming silver lining. You look forward to every day and cherish each moment.

I was fortunate to feel that way for quite some time. When I fell in love with Glen and he in turn loved me, I was grateful. To God. To Glen. To the world. Glen was my whole, wonderful life. I didn't walk; I floated. And I thought I'd float forever.

But one night Glen came home, sat down at our kitchen table, and told me he wanted a divorce. The plate I was drying smashed to the floor. My hands trembled and my eyes filled with tears of horror.

"It's nothing you've done, Darcy. You've been a good wife. It's me. I just don't love you as much as you love me."

"But I love you enough for both of us." My heart was pounding as my mind tried to comprehend what he was saying.

"I know, Darcy. And for a while I've thought that one-way love would be enough for our marriage. But it isn't. I've met someone...someone that I love the way you love me."

My heart splintered at his words. I had been leaning against the sink, and now I slid slowly down to the floor, covering my face with my hands. I sat among the shards of blue stoneware and sobbed.

"I'm not having an affair," he said hoarsely. "I respect both of you too much for that. But every moment I'm with her feels like...like... I want to be with her forever."

He may as well have stabbed me. The feelings that were so familiar to me, feelings I had counted on and treasured, he was experiencing with another woman.

"I'm sorry, Darcy. I did my best to deny my feelings. It's just that my heart won't let me."

"But it's all right to throw my heart on some scrap heap?"

"Please, Darcy, believe me. I never wanted to hurt you." It sounded so hollow. Mostly because it was.

The silence at that moment was suffocating. My hair was standing on end, my fingertips were icy, and I could feel panic filling my entire being. But I couldn't bring myself to speak to him. The only words I could formulate were infused with begging him to love me as much as I loved him.

He spent the night on the couch and was gone from our townhouse in a matter of days. I spent the next few weeks in a cocoon of anger. I was angry with Glen, and I was angry with

God. How could God bring Glen into my life and then take him away? It was cruel—God was cruel. Didn't the desires of my heart have any impact on this all-powerful God? Glen may have thrown it onto the scrap heap, but God was letting my heart stay there.

Glen was always on my mind. I imagined him coming back to me; he would tell me that he only loved her when he thought he couldn't have her. My memories—no, *our* memories—swirled like a tornado in my mind. I embraced them. I loved them.

My best friend noticed my gloomy silences, and one afternoon she said softly, "Darcy, you are so sad. Tell me one thing about your sadness and I'll try to help you with that one thing."

"Glen has forgotten I exist," I blurted out, "and God seems to have written me off, too."

Lisa chose her words very carefully. "Maybe it's the other way around. Maybe Glen was so important to you that *you* pushed God out of the picture."

Her words stung. I inhaled deeply and closed my eyes. When had I last gone to church? I don't remember when I stopped reading the Bible every day.

That night I curled up on my bed and picked up my Bible. It fell open to Matthew 10:39: "Those who find their life will lose it, and those who lose their life for my sake will find it."

The verse stuck in my mind. I mulled it over for weeks. Which turned into months. I had put so much emphasis on my marriage that there was little room for anything else. Once I had what I wanted in life, I had become indifferent to God. There were no more lengthy prayer sessions for help in finding the husband of my dreams. I'd let go of church and church friends. The reason my life was so empty without Glen was because I had made it that way. Glen hadn't, nor had God.

Eventually I realized that in losing the life I'd had with Glen, the Lord was able to lead me back to himself. And it was a much fuller, contented life. I came to see that there had been more fantasy in my marriage than reality. Glen could never have loved me enough. The kind of love I needed could only come from God. Pure, undemanding, and everlasting.

Knowing that God will never leave me... that's the best news for a woman who had left her heart on a scrap heap.

—LORENA O'CONNOR

Jerry Schemmel's Story

"Come to me all you who labor and are heavy laden, and I will give you rest."

—MATTHEW 11:28

On July 19, 1989, United Airlines Flight 232 out of Denver crashed in Sioux City, Iowa. It was a scene played repeatedly on national television. After seeing the destruction, one wonders how anyone could possibly have lived through it. Of the 296 people onboard, 112 perished, but, somehow, 184 made it through the ordeal alive. Jerry Schemmel was one of those survivors, and it changed his life forever.

Jerry was the deputy commissioner and legal counsel of the Continental Basketball Association. Jay Ramsdell, his good friend and boss, was the league's commissioner. The two were on their way to the CBA's college draft in Columbus, Ohio, with a stopover in Chicago.

Running late, they rushed to Denver's old Stapleton Airport only to find that their 7:00 A.M. flight had been canceled—and the next four flights were filled. Jerry and Jay were put on standby. At 12:45 P.M., they got the last two available seats on United Airlines Flight 232. Jerry was given a ticket for Row 23, Jay Row 30. The noisy plane was filled to the brim.

Over north-central Iowa, about 150 miles from Sioux City, the unthinkable happened. There was an onboard explosion. Engine No. 2 was wiped out, taking with it the entire hydraulic system. The plane should have been unflyable, but against all odds the cockpit crew managed to regain some control of the crippled aircraft.

"The plane was veering to the right and circled the small airport in Sioux City 13 times," Jerry recalled. "We came in with an air speed of 255 mph. The normal landing for a DC–10 is 125 mph. The rate of descent was ten times the normal amount. We were told 45 minutes before impact to expect to crash, and there was very little confidence for landing safely and walking off."

Right before they hit, he remembers the cockpit captain announcing to the passengers: "I'm not going to kid anybody—this is going to be rough. This is going to be tougher than anything you've ever been through." Thirty seconds before touchdown, the captain gave the command, "Brace, brace, brace."

"The plane hit the edge of the runway with its right wing first," Jerry said. "There was a lot of chaos: bodies being thrown about, smoke and fire, unrecognizable debris being thrown everywhere. The plane then cartwheeled forward and slid upside down and broke apart, veering into a cornfield."

Jerry was hanging upside down, still strapped in his seat, when his part of the plane came to rest. Badly shaken, Jerry had no idea whether he was dead or alive. Only when fire burned a knuckle on his hand did he fully realize that he had survived. Unbuckling his seat belt, he dropped onto the ceiling.

As he backed away from the fire, he heard two men behind him. One of them said, "Let's start helping some people and maybe we can find a way out in the process." As the three began helping other survivors, they glimpsed a ray of sunlight through the smoke, and they inched their way out of the plane.

Jerry said that what happened next was a matter of instinct. "When I got out, I heard a baby crying. The next thing I knew, I was back inside the wreckage." He found an 11-month-old girl wedged inside an overhead compartment. "I gathered her up and ran back outside thinking the plane would explode, which was the first time I weighed the risk of what I did."

Unfortunately, Jerry's friend, Jay, did not survive. He had been sitting in Row 30, which was about where the plane had broken apart. It took four days to identify his body.

Jerry recovered physically, but he battled post-traumatic stress disorder, anguishing through overwhelming periods of guilt and depression. Jay had died, as did a one-year-old boy sitting in front of Jerry. Before the explosion, Jerry had been playing peekaboo with the child. The randomness—and unfairness—of who lived and who died haunted him. He couldn't feel grateful for his life because he felt guilty for being alive.

His career, which had once been the most important thing in his life, seemed pointless. He was in a downward spiral and couldn't see a glimmer of hope. He stopped returning phone calls, even to his family.

His wife, Diane, had unwavering Christian faith. When she encouraged Jerry to reach out to God, he shut her off. But her consistent strength and courage slowly began to touch his heart. He found himself wondering if God could help him.

"I was sitting in my chair one evening, ten months after the crash, when I realized, for the first time in my life, I couldn't get back up on my own," Jerry admitted. At that low point, with no answers in sight, he began to pray. He asked God to help him, to come into his life and to lift him back up.

Jerry also started reading the Bible. He read a passage in Matthew that pierced his loneliness and calmed his fears: "Come to me all you who labor and are heavy laden, and I will give you rest." For ten months, Jerry had been longing for rest, and now he realized that Jesus promised to provide it.

With that verse firmly planted in his mind, Jerry turned the corner away from the crash and toward all that God had for him. His priorities changed. Christian convictions and focusing on Jesus replaced career goals. His family also took priority over his once all-consuming job.

Jerry is now the voice of the Denver Nuggets, and doing play-by-play is still incredibly exciting. But whether they win or lose is now way down on his list of things that matter.

Jerry says he goes back to that life-changing Bible passage every day and remembers relief flooding over him when he let Jesus lift his burden. It took a plane crash to open his eyes and his heart to the love and rest that Jesus can bring. He hopes it won't take such dire circumstances before others can find it as well.

—RICH BRIGGS

*W*e love because
he first loved us.
—1 JOHN 4:19

Peace That Surpasses All Understanding

While suffering from a serious illness, Alan taught his wife a lesson: Even when we're by ourselves, we are not alone.

I always professed to having faith in God and in his plan for my life, but in the fall of 1998, my strength of faith was tested as never before.

My husband, Alan, and I were extremely happy after 18 years of marriage, and we were enjoying the roller coaster ride that comes with having two teenagers. Our daughter, Jennifer, was a junior in high school, learning to drive and dating her first boyfriend. Our son, Jason, was 15, active in sports, and growing up quickly. My husband was enjoying his work, and after five years of attending night courses at a local college, he was only one semester away from the completion of his dream. We had so much to be grateful for, and we thanked God often for his many blessings.

In September 1998, Alan complained about some pain across his lower back. Within a few

weeks, the pain had increased, spreading to his left side. He was examined by our family physician, who felt that it was probably nothing more than a muscle strain.

Months passed, and Alan began to feel extremely fatigued. Initially we thought working full-time, combined with night classes and other activities, was catching up with him. Then, as the fatigue increased, an inexplicable weight loss began. Repeated visits to the family physician failed to result in a conclusive diagnosis. The weight loss continued, and the fatigue began to restrict Alan's activities. In November, returning to the family doctor, we requested to see a specialist or have more extensive diagnostic tests done.

The doctor ordered a CAT scan, but it couldn't be done until after the Thanksgiving weekend. We tried to enjoy the holiday dinner with our family, but by this time Alan was too weak to enjoy much of anything. Anxiety was mounting within me.

The week after Thanksgiving, Alan had the CAT scan, and then we headed home. We hadn't been there long when the phone rang—it was our doctor. I felt an immediate sense of panic. Even before my husband hung up the phone, tears were streaming down my face. The doctor wanted to see us right away in his office.

As we waited for his name to be called at the doctor's office, Alan kept assuring me that whatever it was, we could deal with it. Once we were seated in his private office, the doctor told us that the CAT scan had revealed a large tumor on Alan's left kidney. It turned out to be malignant. The cancer was at a very advanced stage, and we would need to see a surgeon immediately.

So began the darkest period in my life. The prognosis wasn't good, and the risks involved in the surgery were high. I realized that everything I believed in would now be put to the test. Daily, I claimed every promise from God's word that I had ever been taught, but I found little peace as I contemplated a future that might not include the one person most dear to me. Many sleepless nights I cried out to God and begged to feel his presence with me.

One evening, just a few days before the surgery, I was helping my husband get into bed for the night. I covered him, prayed with him, and turned out the light. As I was leaving the room, I felt a heavy sadness at seeing him lying there alone in the dark. I called out to him, "Alan, are you scared to be left alone in here?"

Alan's reply was simple, but his words would carry me through the many difficult days that were ahead. He answered, "Colleen, I'm *not* alone in here." It was then that I knew all those promises were real. God promises us that he will provide a peace that surpasses all understanding. Alan's words reassured me that this promise had indeed been kept.

With two major surgeries behind us and months of chemotherapy, scans, and uncertainty in front of us, I, too, know something of this peace. Although rough times come and tears sometimes flow, I know I'm not alone. God's faithfulness and provisions have repeatedly confirmed my faith in his promises. Philippians 4:7 is real in our lives as God continues to give us a peace that "surpasses all understanding, [which] will guard your hearts and your minds in Christ Jesus."

—COLLEEN ARMSTRONG

*D*o not worry about
anything, but in everything
by prayer and supplication with
thanksgiving let your requests
be made known to God.

—PHILIPPIANS 4:6

We not only live among men,
but there are airy hosts,
blessed spectators, sympathetic
lookers-on, that see and know
and appreciate our thoughts
and feelings and acts.

—HENRY WARD BEECHER,
ROYAL TRUTHS

Angels
Among Us

An Ordinary Guy

Those with physical challenges can live happy, wonderful lives—especially if their faith in God is strong.

I have this kid who's always been accident-prone. From the time he was a toddler, spring announced its arrival by our first trip of the year to the emergency room: for stitches, bandages, and body casts. The big one came along when he was a teenager.

On one average summer afternoon, the phone rang. Without any foreboding, I casually picked up the phone. Looking back, I want to yell at myself like in the movies, when you see the hero approach danger and you warn loudly: *Look out! Don't pick up that phone!*

"Mrs. Z, Larry fell off his bike and cut himself." I sighed, picked up a towel, and headed to the scene of the accident. Suffice to say, that phone call was certainly understated. It was bad. Very bad.

The next morning, I woke to a cheerful sun and chirping birds and a darkness in my heart that nothing could brighten. Somehow, I knew that my son's life had changed forever. The accident had left him facially disfigured, and multiple skull fractures had his life in jeopardy. His future flashed before me. I wept and went far from God.

That was 25 years ago. I'm amazed how accurate my motherly intuition was. On the other hand, it's astounding how wrong I was...how it all turned out.

Larry's recovery was slow and daunting, yet he forged ahead. After months of surgeries and therapy, he managed to return to the baseball field. His first day back on the pitcher's mound, he got smacked right in the face by the ball. His coach fainted. With blood streaming from his re-broken nose, Larry ran over to the coach and comforted the poor man. I think he pitched a no-hitter that day.

Larry continued to laugh with his friends, tease his sisters, and live normally. He was good and he was bad. And I watched.

At age 19 his seizures began. I was embarrassed for him. He was not. Meningitis set in during his second year of college. The minute he came out of the coma, he walked unassisted to the bathroom when no one was looking. He joked with the nurses and comforted little sick kids. He lost a little something, though, and never did go back to college. Yet over the years—resilient as ever—he continued to work and play and never mentioned the ringing in his ears. I waited.

Finally, he met a sweet young woman who loved him dearly and gave him two little girls. A steady job, a small house in the country—life couldn't be better. Everyone Larry met enjoyed his funny antics and tricks. Then he became friends with a young preacher. As I had turned further from God, Larry turned closer. And closer. God was truly with him, I was beginning to see. He grew better, not bitter. Could I do less?

Conscientious about responsibilities and bills, he happily guided his family frugally and affectionately while ignoring his ringing ears and the dizzy attacks that caught him unaware. Eventually, there was no choice. He had to have ear surgery, which left him partially deaf and paralyzed on one side of the face, including his eye. Larry was now permanently disabled.

Children in church turned and stared.

He prayed, then quickly rebounded to find joy in his children's homework and pleasure in church activities, especially playing pranks on the preacher's wife. I saw him bend to the curb and whisper in an old man's ear. I watched as he shook out the last dollar in his wallet and check his pockets for more to hand to a traveler in need. Angry teens relied on his tender patience. Like a Pied Piper, his joyful spirit led them to hope. He taught me bravery, determination, how to get up when I fall, how to trust, and how to pray—with thanksgiving.

Last year we went to the Christmas play at Larry's church. The lights dimmed and the audience became silent. A deep voice behind the closed curtain began to sing, "I once was lost…" softly, clearly, gently. I had never heard my son sing quite like that before; every tone perfect, the emotion so pure. A bit later, in accordance with the theme of the play, a raucous, unkempt old drunk staggered down the aisle. The audience roared with laughter. My son—the actor. Later in the play, as a pleading penitent, Larry's honest portrayal brought the crowd to tears.

What was going on here? Why was he so good, his singing so lovely, his acting so true? Anxiety stirred deep within me. Perhaps he was leaving. Briefly, eulogies formed in my mind while my heart fought with my head. Then, for the first time in years, I remembered to pray. Within moments, a soft blanket of peace billowed over me, and I settled with a smile to trust. This special night was simply a gift—an evening to remember.

During his storms, like the willow tree, Larry sways and bends until, calm again, he stands tall and majestic. People smile at the infinite beauty in his cheerful heart. Some say, "Why me?" Humbly, my son says, "Why not?"

Who knows why bad things happen to good people? It takes a lot of scrubbing to have a nice shiny floor, and a knife cannot be sharp without vigorous honing. Perhaps injury and injustice are the solvents that clean our souls, that shape and make a man or a woman.

In ancient days, God set saints upon the earth for our example. Today he gives us ordinary people who do ordinary things in extraordinary ways.

—LYNNE ZIELINSKI

Return to Faith

Though life can be hard and people cruel, the Lord is always there with open arms.

*U*nlike some people, I do not like to talk about myself because my past holds some very painful memories. Talking about them brings the emotions back, and they're too hard to deal with.

I've had a hard life. My parents divorced when I was only five years old. My father and stepmother raised me. I didn't see my mother very often while growing up, which devastated me. My father would call the police when she tried to visit me, and it would cause such a scene that my mother decided it was better not to come around. Neither understood the effect this had on me. As a child, I believed I must have been a very bad girl for God to take away my mommy. I only truly began to understand why this happened when I had my own children.

To add to my low self-esteem, I experienced abuse from a family member. Eventually, I came to believe that I deserved all of it. And when a teacher made unwanted advances toward me, it pushed me over the edge. I thought God had deserted me.

My father did one thing right while I was growing up; I'll always thank him for it. He took me to our neighborhood Baptist church. Through this church, I do believe I found the strength of God to survive my many trials. Though I survived my teen years, I was very angry with God. As an adult, I pulled away from my faith as I ventured into the world. I turned away from church. I believed God was punishing me for something I had done. In my heart I felt I wasn't good enough to go to church.

As the years went by, I married, had a son, Daniel, and a daughter, Crystal, but I just felt I was playing house. My husband drank and had other problems, and our marriage fell apart after ten years of trying to make it work. I still refused to return to my faith, blaming God for another of my failures.

It was not much later that I fell in love with a man named Walter. I wasn't looking for another relationship so soon, but I couldn't fight the feelings he awoke inside me. We were both running scared from bad relationships, but we fell in love and there seemed to be no escaping it. We soon found ourselves with a little red-haired son, Billy. Marriage seemed out of the picture since neither of us wanted to be hurt that way again. After both coming out of bad relationships, we somehow made a great team against the world. We related and understood each other because of those failed relationships.

We met in Florida and moved to Houston, which I hated but that was where his job was. When we moved to Mississippi, it felt more like home; we settled right in. Our children loved the schools, and Walter found a good job. I began dedicating more time to my children. I still felt something was missing and kept searching for what it was.

One day my phone rang. I don't remember the exact day, but I remember the call. I always will. A man introduced himself as Mark Hayman. He explained that he was a minister and that he was calling people and do a survey. I answered his questions, and we struck up a bit of conversation. He told me he was the minister at a Baptist church in Pearlington, Mississippi. He then invited me to visit, since I had mentioned that I had been a Baptist. Later I found that he had picked my name out of the telephone book. I believe it was God's will that he was led to me. I was part of God's master plan.

It took awhile, but God and the Holy Spirit were working on me, and I felt that pull, a need that I didn't understand at the time. I tried a few churches closer to me, but they just didn't feel right. I kept coming back to the phone call and the memory of the nice Baptist minister from Pearlington. I wanted to talk to him again and find out more about his church. I searched the phone book and found the number. When I called, I wasn't sure I had the right church, but I left a message on the machine anyway. Reverend Mark returned my message. I asked him all the questions I had, then got directions to get there.

A few weeks later, I pulled myself out of bed on a Sunday morning, got the children moving, and went to his church. I can't explain the feeling I had as I joined that church that morning, but it felt like coming home. It was like we always belonged. The minister's wife made me feel so welcomed. Her hug changed my life. The people were so loving and accepting, and we all received many hugs that morning. My children resisted at first, but I stayed committed. Every Sunday and some Wednesdays we returned. Walter started coming along, too.

It was not long before my daughter went before the church and accepted the Lord Jesus Christ into her life. I was so proud of her, and as I stood up there beside her, I decided to rededicate my life to Jesus. Then my oldest son was saved soon after. My heart was overjoyed to see him stand with the minister in front of everyone and commit his life to Jesus.

Our first Christmas with this church was so special. Knowing our needs, they brought baskets of food and presents. This was the first Christmas I wasn't depressed due to their wonderful show of love. I had spent many Christmases crying because of my unhappy past. These people gave with such Christian love. They showed us what Christmas was all about: Jesus Christ!

Then in February, on Billy's birthday, Walter and I stood before the Lord and the whole church and were married. Our children were in the ceremony, as we lit candles to show family unity. God showered us with his blessings that day.

Since then, my oldest boy helped a friend of his find the Lord also. My mother has started attending church, and much of our family has visited our church. The youth group keeps my children's attention on positive things. Daniel and Crystal are in the choir, and, oh, what beautiful songs they sing. Many people have complimented them on their voices, but they give God the glory.

I have returned to my faith and brought along my family. I now know God wasn't punishing me. He was preparing me and making me a stronger person. He was making me a person who could be a good Christian mother, wife, and woman. I have so much more to learn and much that I must improve on, but with God's help, I know he'll see me through.

I want to be a good example to my children and then, someday, when God calls me home to be with him, I'll be able to say I did my best to raise my children in the way of the Lord. His will is all worked out, and all I have to do is make the right choices. I know God blesses the people who follow his will. He surely has blessed me!

—Judith O'Brien-Beck

Roadside Rescue

Angels come in all varieties—including bikers with scraggly beards and torn blue jeans.

*I*t's a good thing the summer wedding was beautiful, because the rest of the day held nothing but problems. My friend John and I had borrowed my dad's car to attend the wedding of a college friend 150 miles away. Shortly after our venture began, John discovered he had forgotten his wallet at home. Later, at the restaurant, I realized I had left my driver's license in the jeans I'd worn the night before. Then, on the way home, John got really sick. He took out his contacts and slumped in the seat next to me, holding his stomach and looking pale.

That's when the car died at the side of the interstate.

Over and over again, I turned the key, pumped the accelerator, and rocked with the sound of the groaning engine.

"Where's my guardian angel when I need her?" I moaned. Dad had recently shared with Mom and me two books he had received on angels working in our lives. Each of the stories was fascinating and believable. I always knew I had a guardian angel, yet I questioned if I'd ever personally experienced her presence.

"It's seven," John said, squinting at his watch. "We'd better walk back to that gas station before it closes."

I led my visually impaired, nauseated friend down the shoulder of the highway. It was hard to tell if he was sweating from the 96-degree heat or from his fever. My white high heels clicked on the pavement, and the strand of

imitation pearls clung to my neck as we trudged along the roadside.

I called Dad and listened to his mechanical advice. If his suggestions didn't work, I'd have to call a tow truck.

"It's 7:15," Mom said into the speaker phone. "If you aren't back on the road in one hour, call again so we know how you're doing." She tried not to worry about me now that I was in college, but at times like these I knew she couldn't help it.

John and I plodded back down the scorching pavement to the car and tried Dad's long-distance advice. The car coughed and choked but refused to start.

I draped myself over the steering wheel. "What if no one stops to help us?"

"What if someone does?" John worried out loud. He propped his aching head on the dashboard while we swapped tales of horrible crimes that had happened along the highway.

At 7:50, we admitted our defeat and traipsed across the highway to walk back to the gas station. Just then, a white dilapidated station wagon sputtered to a stop in front of our car. I could see the two male occupants through the missing rear window. The driver's long, stringy hair touched the shoulders of his ragged shirt. As we stood across the road from them, John and I agreed that they looked pretty rough.

"And we look pretty rich," John said, motioning to our wedding attire. "Think they'll believe we're poor college students?"

"Need some help?" the driver hollered. His smile leered through his scraggly beard. "I know some 'bout cars." As we headed back across the interstate, we could see that the sleeves had been torn from the denim jacket the man was wearing. His tall leather moccasins had fringe hanging just beneath the knees of his torn blue jeans.

"I always knew my guardian angel would be unique," I teased in a whisper. "Maybe he'll help us."

"Or rob us," John cautioned as we crossed the highway.

A second unshaven man silently exited the car. I thanked them both for stopping and, with trembling hands, released the hood, hoping I wasn't making a big mistake by letting them help us.

The driver bent over the car engine. I read the back of his worn jacket: "Christian Motor-

cycle Association." John and I beamed at each other. I nodded and winked—and breathed a sigh of relief.

Within minutes, the car was running and the four of us stood together smiling and shaking hands. John and I each offered them the only money we had with us: five dollars each, some of it in change. They accepted it gratefully, saying it was more than they'd had in a long time.

I drove home, collapsed in the chair, and recounted my "guardian angel" story to my parents.

Mom's face was serious. "What time did they stop?"

I thought for a minute. "About ten minutes to 8:00."

She smiled at Dad. "I looked at my watch at 7:50 and said to Dad, 'Let's pray an angel stops to help her.'"

Dad said, "That's when I sent you mine."

—LeAnn Thieman

Faith Connects Us to Love

God gives us faith as a means of getting in touch with his love. For once we have that love, we can pass it on to others.

Again, truly I tell you,
if two of you agree on earth
about anything you ask,
it will be done for you
by my Father in heaven.
For where two or three are
gathered in my name,
I am there among them.

—MATTHEW 18:19–20

Community
of Faith

Halfway Home

Children of divorced parents, siblings Sam and Rebekah almost severed their own relation-ship—until God gave them a push.

"*A*re they twins?" people asked Sam and Rebekah's parents.

"No," they said, "just brother and sister 11 months apart."

That was the only time they had been apart. As soon as Sam could crawl over to Rebekah, they were inseparable growing up in their small, neighborly California seaside town.

Both had coppery red hair, freckles, long legs made just for tree climbing and running, and tempers that were spectacular but short-lived.

Their lives were like parallel train tracks. They finished one another's sentences, con-cocted a secret code, and built a clubhouse beneath the flowery hedge at the back of their yard. They even shared a dog, who fortunately had a big enough heart for both.

They were baptized together, he in a little white suit, she in a long-skirted dress, which became grass-stained as soon as they were released to play in the church yard. Pastor Janet had no doubt, however, that both children understood at least the intent of the service, for as Rebekah said, speaking for them both, God was watching over them. "God tells us what to do," she said matter-of-factly. And Pastor Janet believed that, too. She hoped she got to see what God had in store for them.

In the meantime, they learned to swim in the ocean, ride the beginner's waves, and excel in school—some suspected by doing each other's homework. And in the Christmas pageant at their church, they both insisted on being shepherds so they could bring their dog. Since no one could prove that girls weren't shepherds, they carried their cardboard shepherd staffs and led their dog down the aisle three years in a row. Everyone agreed that God must surely have something special in mind for these two. And no one even considered that they might not do it together.

"Forever," they swore, agreeing, using the secret handshake. "We are forever friends."

Sam was the first, of course, to notice that Rebekah was changing. He searched his mind for something that he might have done to annoy her. Maybe she was worried about school, he thought. Girls in seventh grade were pretty weird, he had noticed from his vantage point in sixth grade. Not that everything was always easy, but at least with guys you knew where you stood.

One day, he followed Rebekah from school, keeping her in sight as she rode her blue bicycle rapidly down the coastal path. She wasn't upset when she saw him and the picnic of packaged cupcakes and orange juice that he'd brought. They sat on their favorite part of the beach, a wide expanse of sand broken only by the dune where they were sitting.

Both were too young to be faced with the secret Rebekah had overheard: Their parents were divorcing.

Within months, the house was sold, the flowery clubhouse began overgrowing with weeds, and friends said goodbye. With a finality as swift as the pounding of the "For Sale" sign into the front yard and the judge's gavel severing their parents' marriage and mandating co-custody, childhood was over.

For part of the time, they lived with their mother in a small apartment. They had only east windows, meaning they could never see the ocean on the horizon. They traveled like nomads between campfires, from Mom's

cramped apartment to their father's hillside
estate in lush farming country. His new wife
was sweet but sly, and soon seeds of disruption
were planted.

"But maybe she's right," Sam argued with
Rebekah, whose loyalty to her mother never
wavered. "Maybe Mom drove Dad away with
her silly ideas and dumb plans. Remember how
mad he got when she went back to college?"

"Well, she needed to finish her degree so
she could teach," Rebekah countered.

"Well, Dad says his new wife knows how to be a proper one...staying home with the children and not trying to interfere in his business."

Rebekah stared at her brother. He was a stranger, this sharp-tongued critic.

"You're like the parrot Pastor Janet has. It will say whatever it's told. Dad and *she* are just using you to cause trouble."

Suspecting that she might be right, but unable to bear the thought, Sam walked away from Rebekah, turning his back on her for the first time in their lives.

"He said" versus "she said" was played with an intensity that drowned out everything else...especially their pain and the lostness they felt from all that had been familiar, hopeful, promising—and, as Pastor Janet feared—from the God they'd so confidently placed their trust in.

High school was the turning point, as opposing attitudes turned into vastly different behaviors. When one wasn't in trouble, the other was so often that finally Sam went to live with his father and his new family, expanded now to include two new children.

"My *real* sisters," he said to Rebekah the day he left their mother's house. "I don't care if I ever see you again."

From time to time, though, there would be a flicker of remembrance of their special relationship. They tried, they really did, not to argue at holidays when they were forced together. Often, however, it was more cold war than peace.

Still, it was evident to some of those watching that God had other plans for them.

In an uncanny coincidence—although as Pastor Janet pointed out, "Einstein said that coincidence is God's way of remaining anonymous"—each sent the other a box of packaged cupcakes during the same week, their peace offerings crossing in the mail.

They, too, if asked individually, retained the sense that God had plans for them other than this distance. Although both were faith-filled in their own ways, they couldn't bridge the gap. They quarreled when together at family gatherings, each clinging to a different version of What Had Happened to the Family. Of all the words they flung at one another, the two most glaringly missing were "I'm sorry."

At Rebekah's wedding, Sam sat in the back row and left on the first notes of the recessional, although he thought he might really like her new husband.

Sam couldn't believe it when he got the invitation for Christmas dinner at Rebekah's home. The note was formal and polite... except for the tiny illustration she had added in the swirl of her signature: a freckled smiley-face.

No way, he said, tossing the offending note in the trash. He would have to fly 2,000 miles and eat crow instead of turkey, which he was

sure Rebekah wanted to feed him. For time
had proven their mother's strength and their
father's weakness…especially when it came to
telling the truth. Sam kept only minimal rela-
tions with his father and was trying to work up
the courage to approach his mother. And
Rebekah.

But now, he insisted to himself, was neither
the time nor season to do it, although something was nudging him to make peace. Pastor
Janet, he smiled to himself, might say that God
had once again placed a hand firmly on Sam's
back and was ready to shove!

Sam wasn't coming. Rebekah reread his
note before tossing it in the basket with Christmas cards. He had sent it with a carton of
packaged cupcakes. Her husband had been as
baffled by the gift as he was by her tears at the
sight of it. At least, thank God, she thought
now, Sam still had his sense of humor. And he
remembered the good times. She was glad that
she'd listened to that still, small voice nagging
her to send him the invitation.

But perhaps distance *is* best, Rebekah
decided, trying to put on a bright face as she
hung a holiday wreath on her front door.

Perhaps not, Sam reconsidered, making
secret flight reservations.

Christmas Eve lunch was ready to be served at Rebekah's, and the rest of the family sat at the table. A knock on her door, and suddenly there was Sam: brother, comrade, friend.

Who would presume to explain what urged Sam to venture, or Rebekah to invite, except that love is a map between people in all sorts of relationships, drawn by an insistent God whose plans include, always, reconciliation. At the intersections on this road of grace-filled hope, family members become companions in healing.

As they decided later that day, they had been all along guided by their faith in a hands-on God, which was as stubborn as their other traits, until at last they found reconciliation like a special gift beneath the holiday tree.

—MARGARET ANNE HUFFMAN

*M*ay the God of hope fill
you with all joy and peace in
believing, so that you may
abound in hope by the
power of the Holy Spirit.

—ROMANS 15:13

It Is Well With My Soul

When peace like a river,
   attendeth my way,
When sorrows like sea billows
   roll;
Whatever my lot, Thou hast
   taught me to say,
It is well, it is well with my soul.

It is well with my soul,
It is well, it is well with my soul.

And, Lord, haste the day when
   my faith shall be sight,
The clouds be rolled back as a
   scroll,
The trump shall resound and the
   Lord shall descend,
"Even so"—it is well with my
   soul.

—HORATIO G. SPAFFORD

Never Walk Alone

Barbara thought she was alone in her pew—until she stretched out her arms and felt the grasp of God.

*B*arbara always believed she was a good Christian. She was raised as such, and she had reached the point where she honestly thought she had her spiritual life in order. She believed in God, went to church, and tried to do the right thing. She seemed to be an all-around religiously correct person.

Barbara raised her children the same way she'd been raised. They went to church and attended Bible school. Barbara had the perfect Christian family. Or did she?

Barbara's husband was not interested in church or religion or the idea of a belief in a "higher power." As time went on, he became less "neutral" about his beliefs and actually started to speak out against the idea of Christian beliefs.

The reality of Barbara's belief system began to be strained. She knew that she was following some enlightened path, but she began to have doubts as to what it actually was. Attending church alone began to wear her down emotionally. Each week she would muster up the energy to prepare the children for Sunday services, only to be met by moans and groans of, "Why do we have to go if Daddy doesn't?"

It became an ongoing battle, and by the time she finally dropped the children off at Sunday school, Barbara was more drained than ever. Each week it took more and more effort to become part of the congregation. What made it even more difficult was that they lived in a small community, and the absence of her spouse was obvious.

Couples arrived at church *together,* Barbara observed, unless, of course, they had no spouse. It probably was not as evenly divided as it seemed, but at that point it appeared to her that everyone was happy, joyous, and showing up to church together with love in their hearts.

That was something Barbara wanted more than anything. She wanted to arrive at church with her husband by her side and share the weekly religious experience with him. But the chance of this taking place was next to none, and Barbara knew it.

She continued to participate in the activities of her church and took on a full religious schedule. She taught classes for the second graders, headed up a community action group for her block, served on the church council, and did Bible readings once a month from the pulpit.

So what was missing? Why did Barbara always feel a void? There was a void because her husband did not share her enthusiasm. There was a void because she was always rushing around and getting nowhere. There was a void because as much as she *believed* and *attended* and *did,* something spiritual was missing. However, she did not know that.

She did not know the difference between religion and spirituality. She did not even know there was a difference. Barbara was becoming miserable, and she had no idea why.

She talked about God. She talked about believing. She talked about praying. But she did not really know how to pray, or to believe, or to walk with God. She assumed that if she just continued to do what she believed was right, she was right.

Barbara's idea of praying was to bargain: "If I do this, God, will you do that?" Unfortunately, she did not realize that God does not make deals. In fact, he says as much in the Lord's Prayer: "Thy kingdom come, Thy will be done." Thy will be done? Whose will?

Not Barbara's will. She did not understand, until one Sunday when the true power of spirituality was revealed to her. She took her children to Sunday school, as usual. She sat in church, as usual. Yet no one chose to sit around her. There were the typical perfect-looking couples everywhere. She felt deserted and miserable and alone.

She began praying with her typical, "Dear God, please make me happy, send my husband to church, make my children do well in school, etc." Barbara spent a lot of time telling God what to do. She never realized that God likes to be in charge of the plans he's laid out.

In Barbara's church, the Lord's Prayer is a meaningful, community-connected prayer.

Everyone holds hands and recites it together, as one. Unfortunately for Barbara, there was no one sitting next to her on either side. There was no one even close enough in front of or behind her to reach across the benches. This was an unusual morning, and Barbara was feeling particularly alone.

As the congregation recited the prayer, holding hands, Barbara simply stretched out her arms, palms up, and joined in the recitation. As she prayed, a strange sensation took hold of her. She felt her hand being grasped. She felt a tiny jolt running through her body, and the hair on her arms began to tingle. She found herself lost in the prayer.

At the completion, she looked around, searchingly, for the person who had moved next to her to grasp her hand. No one was there; no one was on either side of her. No one had moved to the front or back of her. She still stood alone, but she was not alone. Someone had held her hand. Someone was there to keep her company. Someone was showing her the difference between showing up for church and having the inner peace of knowing what it is like to have the spirit with her.

Barbara was fraught with emotion; she did not know what to do next. But she didn't have to do anything. She was filled with peace. She was overjoyed. She knew she had been filled with something she could never provide on her own. The Spirit truly acknowledged her and she, in turn, realized what it meant when she said, "Thy will be done."

That day, Barbara learned that she does not have to have someone physically sitting next to her. Her husband does not have to attend church with her, and her children do not have to be perfect academic specimens. That's not what is important. She still works diligently for the church and its many projects—her basic routine hasn't changed much. However, Barbara knows it is not her will that is giving her direction. She has learned that God is with her

all the time, and it is his will being done. On that Sunday, she finally understood the difference between religion and spirituality. God truly was with her, and he gave her inner peace. She will never walk alone again.

—Elizabeth Toole

Summing It Up

Children sitting at your knee,
Great Teacher, we're collecting
footnotes of faith wisdom:
In prayer, grumbling is good;
in stress, grieving is essential;
and in trouble, redeeming
grace is promised. In that truth,
we'll not drudge through life
but rather fly like skiers down
a powdery slope.

Strength in Numbers

Once mistaking solitude for peace, this solo Christian discovered greater joy when she joined a community of fellow believers.

*I*n my middle age, I was choosing an increasingly solitary path. My children were grown, I was no longer married, and my writing profession is a lonely one. I had a few close friends and did not seek out others. When they invited me to their gatherings, I had lots of excuses for not attending. My church involvement was languishing, as was the rest of my life. I was choosing solitude and calling it peace. My favorite prayer was the St. Francis prayer: "Lord, make me an instrument of thy peace." I prayed it every day because the words were beautiful, and I figured it couldn't hurt.

A move took me far from my home church, and I did not join another. I attended a church of another denomination, arriving just before the choir marched down the aisle and leaving by the side door so that I wouldn't have to talk to anyone. When they passed the peace, I would've preferred they pass the collection plate again. I would have gladly paid twice to avoid those strangers' handshakes and cheerful greetings. The beauty of the music and liturgy seemed to make up for the lack of relationships in this church. When invited to coffee hour, I aired yet another excuse. My "coffee hour" was a walk through the forest preserve, contemplating God's grace.

My goal was more isolation. I wanted to write novels undisturbed by humanity. I could create fictional worlds and not have to deal with the real one. My church attendance became erratic. I stopped writing fiction. I completed my writing assignments with the discipline that comes with years of practice, but the work I love stopped there. Never a TV watcher before, I became a channel surfer. I was still able to minister to my family and friends, but even that seemed to be waning.

A friend suggested a three-day retreat that she had found transforming. I went with some eagerness, expecting to find some direction for what I was finally admitting to be an unfruitful life. During one of the talks, someone used a phrase I had never heard before: "solo Christian." His dire prediction was that "solo Christians are not going to make it."

That was my wake-up call. The next week, I went to my brother's church. I was a stranger for only five minutes. The pastor brought the microphone to guests for introductions. Where once I would have wanted to crawl under the pew, I was pleased, even eager, to introduce myself.

The congregation welcomed two new members that morning, and I envisioned myself in their places. When they faced the congregation and said what gifts they were bringing to their church community, I found myself answering in silence the words I would say when my membership moment arrived.

During coffee hour, people asked me my name, not what I "do." Since the divorce, my persona has been "writer." Having failed at marriage, I was proud at having succeeded in my profession. It had never occurred to me that I could be interesting and acceptable just as myself.

When I joined the church several months later, the gift that I offered was intercessory prayer. My solitary years had taught me how to pray. I prayed often for myself, for world peace, and for my small circle of friends. Now, it was time to include my new community in my prayers. Unlike most of the members, who had family responsibilities, I had big blocks of uninterrupted time in which to intercede for those who asked. Sometimes I was moved to pray for people who did not ask. I never knew the specific problem, just that prayers were needed.

I doubt I made a dent for peace in our broken world, but I began to live the rest of St. Francis's prayer: "Where there is hatred, let me sow love; where there is injury, pardon; where there is doubt, faith; where there is despair, hope; where there is darkness, light; and where there is sadness, joy."

As a solo Christian, I had not been close enough to others to live out this prayer in a meaningful way. In this community, I found many opportunities to sow these good seeds. I developed a love for St. Francis. I aspired to achieve his holiness, I looked to him as a mentor and friend.

A new friend from my church invited me to join her on a trip to Italy, and I accepted happily. In the past I had traveled alone. While in Rome, it became apparent that a trip to Assisi, St. Francis's birthplace, would not be possible. "Next trip," she assured me. I don't know what made me say: "This trip—you'll see."

The next day we were invited by a priest we knew to visit St. Benedict's hermitage in the countryside around Rome. But as we headed out of Rome, he said: "You know, I haven't been to Assisi for a while. Would you mind going there instead?"

We had a beautiful day in Assisi. We saw the famous frescoes in St. Francis's "upper" church, and I lit a candle at his grave in the "lower" church. We stayed until after dark so that we could stroll around the church one last time in the moonlight. It was extraordinarily beautiful. The day was a blessing, a gift; we were all thankful.

That very night, an earthquake struck and damaged St. Francis's church and other parts of Assisi. Many of the beautiful frescoes are now dust, and the upper church is still closed to visitors. It amazes me to realize I was one of the last people to see the frescoes. As a solo Christian, I would not have gone to Italy, much less to Assisi.

I have come to believe that solitude is not a bad thing when it is part of a balanced life. I have sacrificed nothing in my journey back into a church community and a fuller, richer life— and I still have an hour or two a day to write my novel.

—CAROL STIGGER

St. Francis's Prayer

Lord, make me an instrument of
thy peace;
where there is hatred, let me sow
love;
where there is injury, pardon;
where there is doubt, faith;
where there is despair, hope;
where there is darkness, light;
and
where there is sadness, joy.
O Divine Master, grant that I
may not so much seek
to be consoled as to console;
to be understood, as to
understand;
to be loved, as to love;
for it is in giving that we receive;
it is in pardoning that we are
pardoned,
and it is in dying that we are
born to eternal life.

Standing for Something

Inspired by her faith in God, Alana sparked the creation of a different kind of "in crowd."

*F*or high school junior Alana Wilkes, just being friendly, nice, and generous was no longer enough to guarantee popularity. She was one of the best students academically and one of the most liked, with friends in just about every social group at school. People were drawn to her natural good looks, sense of humor, and kind personality, and she was often invited to the hottest parties, no matter which "clique" was involved.

At the final Junior Grad Nite party, Alana got a lesson in the fragility of popularity. The party took place at school, but many kids chose to take off for a separate, unsupervised "get-together." Alana went along, but she became uncomfortable when several kids offered her alcohol. She tried to explain that she didn't drink, hoping that would suffice, but they continued prodding her to "get buzzed" along with everyone else. One girl accused her of being a snob, and a guy she hardly knew tried to get her to smoke pot with him.

Alana refused to drink or do drugs for anyone, knowing that her own values were more important than the approval of her peers. Still, she knew this was not the common position for girls her age. She was sure she would pay a price for it. She refused drink after drink, smoke after smoke, trying to explain her values to anyone who would listen. But nobody seemed to care.

Luckily, she had her own car there and quietly slipped out. At home, she told her mom what had happened. Her mom hugged her, proud to have a daughter with the courage to stand for something good. "You're special," she told Alana, but Alana didn't feel very special, excusing herself to go to bed.

An hour later, her phone rang and her friend Sarah informed her that the "in crowd" was casting her out. Alana could tell that Sarah was drunk, and her stomach ached as she hung up the phone. She prayed to God for strength and guidance, asking him to keep her strong and steady on her path, even in the midst of the temptations to be one of the crowd.

The next day Alana felt as though everyone at school was shunning her. She tried to talk to her usual group of friends, including Sarah, but got the cold shoulder. Many of them had hangovers, and rumors were spreading that two of the more "serious" partiers never even made it home. Alana wanted nothing more than to end her junior year and have the long summer to not have to worry about how popular she was, or wasn't. She could feel a confrontation brewing as she headed toward her locker. She saw Sarah and a group of girls waiting for her.

Alana emptied her locker quietly as Sarah asked accusingly, "So who do you think you are? Better than us?" It was a simple question, simply asked. Alana just shook her head softly. "I'm a child of God and I refuse to destroy my life," she whispered humbly. Then she looked right at Sarah. "If only you could see that you're a child of God, too, Sarah. All of you are."

As Alana walked away, she heard them catcalling and laughing, but she didn't care. She meant every word of what she had said, and her conviction was strong as she left the school, even though she knew she wouldn't be invited to any big parties that summer. As she climbed into her car, a girl in a JV sweater approached and called out, "Hey!" Alana looked at her warily, expecting another show-down, but instead the girl introduced herself with a smile. Alana realized it was Jane Asher, a member of the tennis team and the best student in the junior class.

Jane told Alana that she, too, had been at the Junior Grad Nite party and saw what had gone on. "I totally admire you," Jane told Alana, explaining that she had also left the party after being pressured to drink and smoke. The more the girls talked, the more they found things in common, especially their strong Christian values and their desire to stand up for what they believed in, even if it meant they would suffer for it.

The two made a date to go shopping that weekend, and over the summer they built a strong bond. Jane introduced Alana to her other friends, and they created their own "in crowd," but with one exception. This "in crowd" would never force anyone to drink, do drugs, or go against their own personal beliefs. They weren't the most popular group on campus, but they were the fastest growing, as more and more kids realized that they didn't have to get drunk or get high to have fun. Like Alana, they had begun to realize that the most important thing in life was not to be popular, but to be yourself.

—MARIE JONES

Family Ties

God doesn't expect us to go it alone. Even Jesus recruited 12 apostles.

There was sticky oatmeal smooshed in Rosamond's hair. And, when Andrea finally found her behind the couch in the living room, Rosamond had taken off her shoes and was in the process of removing her socks—for the third time this morning.

Andrea might've laughed to see such a sight had Rosamond been a mischievous toddler instead of a white-haired old lady, her mother, nearly 80 years old.

Rosamond was suffering from what some people misguidedly called "second childhood." There was nothing childish about it, as Andrea knew too well. Alzheimer's disease or senility or dementia or whatever label they used, it was still dreadful, she thought from her spot in the doorway watching her mother struggle to remove her socks.

When your babies dabble in their cereal, the knowledge that they will outgrow such nonsensical behavior lets you smile. When it's your mother finger-painting in the oatmeal, you can only cry, clinging wearily to the faith that promised support. Andrea swiped her tears away with a shirttail and moved to the task of retrieving Grandma from the mess her life had become.

"Dear God," Andrea prayed later, "I'm so tired, and I feel so helpless."

Turning to God wasn't a new thing. Their conversations were just a bit more intense now. And yet it seemed that faith was more about nice thoughts and ideas instead of such tips as how to get oatmeal out of new upholstery and the VCR, her mother's most recent discovery for places to put food. Whatever faith was, Andrea was certain hers was lacking.

"I can't do this anymore," Andrea lamented later when a friend from their Bible study called to invite her for lunch. Did she mean attending the study, eating out, or caring for her mother? All of the above, Andrea admitted when her friend gently prodded.

"Okay, I'll bring you lunch," said her friend. "Go wash your face, set the table with your best china and silver, and stir us up some iced tea."

"My children are being cheated, and I don't want to even think about what this is doing to my marriage," confessed Andrea over lunch, grateful her mother was napping. "I feel so guilty at wanting relief." She was surprised to hear the anger in her voice.

It's guilt that begets anger, Andrea realized as she listened to herself talk to her sympathetic friend. But how can a good daughter be angry and turn her back on her mother?

"My faith must not be strong enough," she said tearfully. "Mother took care of me…all of her five children…so I can't believe I'm feeling so selfish. God must be so disappointed."

"Some days I wish I were an orphan," Andrea complained. "I might as well be, although I have two sisters and two brothers. But they live conveniently far away and aren't around to help."

"Did Jesus do everything alone?" her friend interjected gently.

Andrea was shocked into silence. Finally, she had to shake her head.

"He got at least a dozen people to help out, right? And what did he say about loving others?"

Here, Andrea was on firmer ground. "That's what we are supposed to do," she said firmly. "And I *am* loving my mother."

"And how are we supposed to love others?"

Too late. Andrea saw the trap she'd let herself fall into.

"Okay, okay," she said with a hesitant smile, "I get your point. Love others as yourself."

"And, my friend, as much as I love you, I'm not sure I would want you loving me the way that you are loving yourself!" Her friend laughed, leaning triumphantly back in her chair.

The first thing Andrea did when her friend left was to call and invite her long-distance siblings to come home. Drawing upon her faith, which her friend had fanned like a bellows on embers, she had decided she was going to ask for help.

Jesus didn't feel ashamed about asking for help. He simply did it. And so would she. A month later, she drove to the airport to meet the planes bringing her siblings home.

Once they realized that Andrea wasn't angry, merely tired and overwhelmed, her brothers and sisters pooled their considerable energy and ideas together. They found respite care, home health services, and, most importantly, a chance to tell Andrea what her steadfastness meant to all of them. Finally, as a love gift for Andrea, one of her sisters gave her the name and address of a support group.

"Go, Andrea," she instructed. "If you do that, we promise to come back home regularly." She exchanged smiling glances with her other sister and the brothers. "We've already got it set up so that you and your husband can take a second honeymoon."

"You're my guardian angel," Andrea told her friend after her brothers and sisters had returned to their homes. "You reminded me that my faith is practical, not theoretical."

"Sure, and it can lead you to answers," her friend said, disclaiming the angel label.

It's also a deep taproot, like the one supporting the big, old oak tree in the backyard that mother planted when she was a little girl. Andrea mused about the analogy as she tucked Rosamond in for the night—before the woman they had hired to stay with her arrived.

"There are two halves of the equation, I'm so fond of spouting," she said to herself.

"Except I left out the part God put in for me: Love others as you love yourself."

Fortified with this assurance, Andrea carved out time to soak, at least briefly, in bubble baths. She found time to go on dates with her husband and on roller-skating adventures and long walks to the library with her children.

The coffeepot bubbled softly as Andrea and a dozen men and women gathered in a caring circle. They were members in a club no one had wanted to join: caretakers of aging, infirm parents. Yet, here they gained support for keeping the family intact.

"Both Mom and my own family are getting the best out of me now that I don't have to do it alone, which God never intended," Andrea said. She was grateful to her siblings for doing what they could: supporting, staying involved, and finding this group for her.

She had also realized that her children were a God-given resource right under her nose! All it had taken to get them to help out more with Grandma was to ask. And in the ensuing conversation, Andrea had been surprised to learn what a good thing it meant to them to have Grandma at home.

"If a family sticks together, *everyone* can make it," Andrea assured. "Faith," she added from first-hand knowledge, "provides practicality."

Like an extra pair of hands, she thought gratefully, to gently wash oatmeal out of soft, still-lovely white hair.

—MARGARET ANNE HUFFMAN

*T*hese trials are only to test
your faith, to see whether or not
it is strong and pure. It is being
tested as fire tests gold and
purifies it—and your faith is far
more precious to God than mere
gold; so if your faith remains
strong after being tried in the
test tube of fiery trials, it will
bring you much praise and
glory and honor on the
day of his return.

—1 Peter 1:7 (TLB)